Bilingual Classics

双语经典

贝多芬传

〔法国〕罗曼·罗兰 著

傅雷 译

译林出版社

......故天将降大任于是人也，必先苦其心志，劳其筋骨，饿其体肤，空乏其身，行拂乱其所为，所以动心忍性，曾益其所不能。

——孟子（译者录）

目　录

译者序

唯有真实的苦难，才能驱除罗曼蒂克的幻想的苦难；唯有看到克服苦难的壮烈的悲剧，才能帮助我们担受残酷的命运；唯有抱着"我不入地狱谁入地狱"的精神，才能挽救一个萎靡而自私的民族：这是我十五年前初次读到本书时所得的教训。

不经过战斗的舍弃是虚伪的，不经劫难磨炼的超脱是轻佻的，逃避现实的明哲是卑怯的；中庸，苟且，小智小慧，是我们的致命伤：这是我十五年来与日俱增的信念。而这一切都由于贝多芬的启示。

我不敢把这样的启示自秘，所以十年前就移译了本书。现在阴霾遮蔽了整个天空，我们比任何时候都更需要精神的支持，比任何时候都更需要坚忍、奋斗、敢于向神明挑战的大勇主义。现在，当初生的音乐界只知训练手的技巧，而忘记了培养心灵的神圣工作的时候，这部《贝多芬传》对读者该有更深刻的意义。——由于这个动机，我重译了本书。①

　　此外，我还有个人的理由。疗治我青年时世纪病的是贝多芬，扶植我在人生中的战斗意志的是贝多芬，在我灵智的成长中给我大影响的是贝多芬，多少次的颠扑曾由他搀扶，多少的创伤曾由他抚慰，——且不说引我进音乐王国的这件次要的恩泽。除了把我所受的恩泽转赠给比我年轻的一代之外，我不知还有什么方法可以偿还我对贝多芬，和对他伟大的传记家罗曼·罗兰所负的债务。表示感激的最好的方式，是施予。

　　为完成介绍的责任起见，我在译文以外，附加了一篇分析贝多芬作品的文字。我明知道是一件越俎的工作，但望这番力不从心的努力，能够发生抛砖引玉的作用。

译者
1942 年 3 月

---

① 译注：这部书的初译稿，成于 1932 年，在存稿堆下埋藏了有几十年之久。——出版界坚持本书已有译本，不愿接受。但已出版的译本绝版已久，我始终未曾见到。然而我深深地感谢这件在当时使我失望的事故，使我现在能全部重译，把少年时代幼稚的翻译习作一笔勾销。

原　序

二十五年前，当我写这本小小的《贝多芬传》时，我不曾想要完成什么音乐学的著作。那是 1902 年。我正经历着一个骚乱不宁的时期，充满着兼有毁灭与更新作用的雷雨。我逃出了巴黎，来到我童年的伴侣，曾经在人生的战场上屡次撑持我的贝多芬那边，寻觅十天的休息。我来到波恩，他的故里。我重复找到了他的影子和他的老朋友们，就是说在我到科布伦茨访问的韦格勒的孙子们身上，重又见到了当年的韦格勒夫妇。在美因茨，我又听到他的交响乐大演奏会，是魏因加特纳[①]指挥的。然后我又和他单独相对，倾吐着我的衷曲，在多雾的莱茵河畔，在那些潮湿而灰色的四月天，浸淫着他的苦难，他的勇气，他的欢乐，他的悲哀；我跪着，由他用强有力的手搀扶起来，给我的新生儿约翰·克利斯朵夫[②]行了洗礼；在他祝福之下，我重又

---

①　译注：魏因加特纳（Felix Weingartner，1863—1942），系指挥贝多芬作品之权威。

②　译注：指罗曼·罗兰名著《约翰·克利斯朵夫》，最初数卷的事实和主人翁的性格，颇多取材于贝多芬的事迹与为人。且全书的战斗精神与坚忍气息，尤多受贝多芬的感应。

踏上巴黎的归路，得到了鼓励，和人生重新缔了约，一路向神明唱着病愈者的感谢曲。那感谢曲便是这本小册子。先由《巴黎杂志》发表，后又被贝玑拿去披露。^①我不曾想到本书会流传到朋友们的小范围以外。可是"各有各的命运……"

恕我叙述这些枝节。但今日会有人在这支颂歌里面寻求以严格的史学方法写成的渊博的著作，对于他们，我不得不有所答复。我自有我做史家的时间。我在《亨德尔》和关于歌剧研究的几部书内，已经对音乐学尽了相当的义务。但《贝多芬传》绝非为了学术而写的。它是受伤而窒息的心灵的一支歌，在苏生与振作之后感谢救主的，我知道，这救主已经被我改换面目。但一切从信仰和爱情出发的行为都是如此的。而我的《贝多芬传》便是这样的行为。

大家人手一编地拿了去，给这册小书走上它不曾希望的好运。那时候，法国几百万的生灵，被压迫的理想主义者的一代，焦灼地等待着一声解放的讯号。这讯号，他们在贝多芬的音乐中听到了，他们便去向他呼吁。经历过那个时代的人，谁不记得那些四重奏音乐会，仿佛弥撒祭中唱《神之羔羊》^②时的教堂，——谁不记得那些痛苦的脸，注视着祭献礼，因它的启示而受着光辉的烛照？生在今日的人们已和生在昨日的人们离得远远的了。（但生在今日的人们是否能和生在明日的离得更近？）在本世纪初期的

---

① 译注：贝玑（Charles Peguy，1873—1914），法国近代大诗人，与作者同辈，早亡。本书全文曾在贝玑主编的《半月刊》上发表。
② 译注：此系弥撒祭典礼中之一节。

这一代里，多少行列已被歼灭：战争开了一个窟窿，他们和他们最优秀的儿子都失了踪影。我的小小的《贝多芬传》保留着他们的形象。出自一个孤独者的手笔，它不知不觉地竟和他们相似。而他们早已在其中认出自己。这小册子，由一个无名的人写的，从一家无名的店铺里出来，几天之内在大众手里传播开去，它已不再属于我了。

我把本书重读了一遍，虽然残缺，我也不拟有所更易。①因为它应当保存原来的性质，和伟大的一代神圣的形象。在贝多芬百年祭②的时候，我纪念那一代，同时颂扬它伟大的同伴，正直与真诚的大师，教我们如何生如何死的大师。

罗曼·罗兰

1927 年 3 月

① 作者曾预备另写一部历史性的和专门性的书，以研究贝多芬的艺术和他创造性的人格。

译注：此书早已于 1928 年正月在巴黎出版。

② 译注：1927 年适为贝多芬百年死忌。

初版序

> 我愿证明，凡是行为善良与高尚的人，定能因之而担当患难。

——贝多芬（1819年2月1日在维也纳市政府语）

我们周围的空气多沉重。老大的欧罗巴在重浊与腐败的气氛中昏迷不醒。鄙俗的物质主义镇压着思想，阻挠着政府与个人的行动。社会在乖巧卑下的自私自利中窒息以死。人类喘不过气来。——打开窗子吧！让自由的空气重新进来！呼吸一下英雄们的气息。

人生是艰苦的。在不甘于平庸凡俗的人，那是一场无日无之的斗争，往往是悲惨的，没有光华的，没有幸福的，在孤独与静寂中展开的斗争。贫穷，日常的烦虑，沉重与愚蠢的劳作，压在他们身上，无益地消耗着他们的精力，没有希望，没有一道欢乐之光，大多数还彼此隔离着，连对患难中的弟兄们一援手的安慰都没有，他们不知道彼此的存在。他们只能依靠自己；可是有时连最强的人都不免在苦难中蹉跌。他们求助，求一个朋友。

为了援助他们，我才在他们周围集合一班英雄的友人，一班为了善而受苦的伟大的心灵。这些"名人传"①不是向野心家的骄傲申说的，而是献给受难者的。并且实际上谁又不是受难者呢？让我们把神圣的苦痛的油膏，献给苦痛的人吧！我们在战斗中不是孤军。世界的黑暗，受着神光烛照。即是今日，在我们近旁，我们也看到闪耀着两朵最纯洁的火焰，正义与自由：毕加大佐和布尔民族。②即使他们不曾把浓密的黑暗一扫而空，至少他们在一闪之下已给我们指点了大路。跟着他们走吧，跟着那些散在各个国家、各个时代的孤独奋斗的人走吧。让我们来摧毁时间的阻隔，使英雄的种族再生。

我称为英雄的，并非以思想或强力称雄的人；而只是靠心灵而伟大的人。好似他们之中最伟大的一个，就是我们要叙述他的生涯的人所说的："除了仁慈以外，我不承认还有什么优越的标记。"没有伟大的品格，就没有伟大

---

① 译注：作者另有《米开朗琪罗传》、《托尔斯泰传》，皆与本书同列在"名人传"这总标题内。

② 译注：1894 至 1906 年间，法国有一历史性的大冤狱，即史家所谓"德雷福斯事件"。德雷福斯大尉被诬通敌罪，判处苦役。1895 年陆军部秘密警察长发觉前案系罗织诬陷而成，竭力主张平反，致触怒军人，连带下狱。著名文豪左拉亦以主张正义而备受迫害，流亡英伦。迨 1899 年，德雷福斯方获军事法庭更审，改判徒刑十年，复由大总统下令特赦。1906 年，德雷福斯再由最高法院完全平反，撤销原判。毕加大佐为昭雪此冤狱之最初殉难者，故作者以之代表正义。

布尔民族为南非好望角一带的荷兰人，自维也纳会议，荷兰将好望角割让于英国后，英人虐待布尔人甚烈，卒激成 1899 至 1902 年间的布尔战争。结果英国让步，南非联盟宣告成立，为英国自治领地之一。作者以之代表自由的火焰。

的人，甚至也没有伟大的艺术家，伟大的行动者；所有的只是些空虚的偶像，匹配下贱的群众的：时间会把他们一齐摧毁。成败又有什么相干？主要是成为伟大，而非显得伟大。

这些传记中人的生涯，几乎都是一种长期的受难。或是悲惨的命运，把他们的灵魂在肉体与精神的苦难中磨折，在贫穷与疾病的铁砧上锻炼；或是，目击同胞受着无名的羞辱与劫难，而生活为之戕害，内心为之碎裂，他们永远过着磨难的日子；他们固然由于毅力而成为伟大，可是也由于灾患而成为伟大。所以不幸的人啊！切勿过于怨叹，人类中最优秀的和你们同在。汲取他们的勇气做我们的养料吧；倘使我们太弱，就把我们的头枕在他们膝上休息一会吧。他们会安慰我们。在这些神圣的心灵中，有一股清明的力和强烈的慈爱，像激流一般飞涌出来。甚至无须探询他们的作品或倾听他们的声音，就在他们的眼里，他们的行述里，即可看到生命从没像处于患难时的那么伟大，那么丰满，那么幸福。

在此英勇的队伍内，我把首席给予坚强与纯洁的贝多芬。他在痛苦中间即曾祝望他的榜样能支持别的受难者，"但愿不幸的人，看到一个与他同样不幸的遭难者，不顾自然的阻碍，竭尽所能地成为一个不愧为人的人，而能借以自慰"。经过了多少年超人的斗争与努力，克服了他的苦难,完成了他所谓"向可怜的人类吹嘘勇气"的大业之后，这位胜利的普罗米修斯①，回答一个向他提及上帝的朋友时说道："噢，人啊，你当自助！"

我们对他这句豪语应当有所感悟。依着他的先例，我们应当重新鼓起对生命对人类的信仰！

罗曼·罗兰

1903 年 1 月

---

① 译注：神话中的火神，人类文明最初的创造者。作者常用以譬喻贝多芬。

贝多芬传

贝多芬画像（21 岁）

格哈德·冯·库格根（Gerhard von Kügelgen）微型画创作

竭力为善，

爱自由甚于一切，

即使为了王座，

也永勿欺妄真理。

——贝多芬（1792 年手册）

他短小臃肿，外表结实，生就运动家般的骨骼。一张土红色的宽大的脸，到晚年才皮肤变得病态而黄黄的，尤其是冬天，当他关在室内远离田野的时候。额角隆起，宽广无比。乌黑的头发，异乎寻常的浓密，好似梳子从未在上面光临过，到处逆立，赛似"美杜萨头上的乱蛇"。①眼中燃烧着一股奇异的威力，使所有见到他的人为之震慑；但大多数人不能分辨它们微妙的差别。因为在褐色而悲壮的脸上，这双眼睛射出一道犷野的光，所以大家总以为是黑的；其实却是灰蓝的。②平时又细小又深陷，兴奋或愤怒的时光才大张起来，在眼眶中旋转，那才奇妙地反映出它们真正的思想。③他往往用忧郁的目光向天凝视。宽大的鼻子又短又方，竟是狮子的相貌。一张细腻的嘴巴，但下唇常有比上唇前突的倾向。牙床结实得厉害，似乎可以嗑破核桃。左边的下巴有一个深陷的小窝，使他的脸显得

---

① 以上据英国游历家罗素 1822 年时记载。——1801 年，车尔尼尚在幼年，看到贝多芬蓄着长发和多日不剃的胡子，穿着羊皮衣裤，以为遇到了小说中的鲁滨孙。

译注：美杜萨系神话中三女妖之一，以生有美发著名。后因得罪火神，美发尽变毒蛇。车尔尼（1791—1857）为奥国有名的钢琴家，为肖邦挚友，其钢琴演奏当时与肖邦齐名。

② 据画家克勒贝尔记载，他曾于 1818 年为贝多芬画像。

③ 据医生米勒 1820 年记载：他的富于表情的眼睛，时而妩媚温柔，时而惘然，时而气焰逼人，可怕非常。

古怪地不对称。据莫舍勒斯说："他的微笑是很美的，谈话之间有一副往往可爱而令人高兴的神气。但另一方面，他的笑却是不愉快的，粗野的，难看的，并且为时很短"——那是一个不惯于欢乐的人的笑。他通常的表情是忧郁的，显示出"一种无可疗治的哀伤"。1825 年，雷斯塔伯说看见"他温柔的眼睛及其剧烈的痛苦"时，他需要竭尽全力才能止住眼泪。一年以后，布劳恩·冯·布劳恩塔尔在一家酒店里遇见他，坐在一隅抽着一支长烟斗，闭着眼睛，那是他临死以前与日俱增的习惯。一个朋友向他说话。他悲哀地微笑，从袋里掏出一本小小的谈话手册；然后用着聋子惯有的尖锐的声音，教人家把要说的话写下来。——他的脸色时常变化，或是在钢琴上被人无意中撞见的时候，或是突然有所感应的时候，有时甚至在街上，使路人大为吃惊。"脸上的肌肉突然隆起，血管膨胀；犷野的眼睛变得加倍可怕；嘴巴发抖；仿佛一个魔术家召来了妖魔而反被妖魔制服一般"，那是莎士比亚式的面目。[①]尤利乌斯·贝内迪克特说他无异"李尔王"。[②]

路德维希·凡·贝多芬，1770 年 12 月 16 日生于科隆附近的波恩，一所破旧屋子的阁楼上。他的出身是佛兰芒

① 克勒贝尔说是莪相的面目。以上的细节皆采自贝多芬的朋友，及见过他的游历家的记载。
译注：莪相为三世纪时苏格兰行吟诗人。
② 译注：李尔王系莎士比亚名剧中的人物。

族。①父亲是一个不聪明而酗酒的男高音歌手。母亲是女仆，一个厨子的女儿，初嫁男仆，夫死再嫁贝多芬的父亲。

艰苦的童年，不像莫扎特般享受过家庭的温情。一开始，人生于他就显得是一场悲惨而残暴的斗争。父亲想开拓他的音乐天分，把他当作神童一般炫耀。四岁时，他就被整天地钉在洋琴②前面，或和一架提琴一起关在家里，几乎被繁重的工作压死。他的不致永远厌恶这艺术总算是万幸的了。父亲不得不用暴力来迫使贝多芬学习。他少年时代就得操心经济问题，打算如何挣取每日的面包，那是来得过早的重任。十一岁，他加入戏院乐队；十三岁，他当大风琴手。1787年，他丧失了他热爱的母亲。"她对我那么仁慈，那么值得爱戴，我的最好的朋友！噢！当我能叫出母亲这甜蜜的名字而她能听见的时候，谁又比我更幸福？"③她是肺病死的；贝多芬自以为也染着同样的病症；他已常常感到痛楚；再加比病魔更残酷的忧郁。④十七岁，他做了一家之主，负着两个兄弟的教育之责；他不得不羞

---

① 他的祖父名叫路德维希，是家族里最优秀的人物，生在安特卫普，直到二十岁时才住到波恩来，做当地大公的乐长。贝多芬的性格和他最像。我们必须记住这个祖父的出身，才能懂得贝多芬奔放独立的天性，以及别的不全是德国人的特点。

译注：今法国与比利时交界之一部及比利时西部之地域，古称佛兰德。佛兰芒即居于此地域内之人种名。安特卫普为今比利时西北部之一大城名。

② 译注：洋琴为钢琴以前的键盘乐器，形式及组织大致与钢琴同。

③ 以上见1789年9月15日贝多芬致奥格斯堡地方的沙德医生书信。

④ 他1816年时说："不知道死的人真是一个可怜虫！我十五岁上已经知道了。"

13 岁的贝多芬，1783 年

惭地要求父亲退休，因为他酗酒，不能主持门户：人家恐怕他浪费，把养老俸交给儿子收领。这些可悲的事实在他心上留下了深刻的创痕。他在波恩的一个家庭里找到了一个亲切的依傍，便是他终身珍视的布罗伊宁一家。可爱的埃莱奥诺雷·冯·布罗伊宁比他小两岁。他教她音乐，领她走上诗歌的路。她是他的童年伴侣；也许他们之间曾有相当温柔的情绪。后来埃莱奥诺雷嫁了韦格勒医生，他也成为贝多芬的知己之一；直到最后，他们之间一直保持着恬静的友谊，那是从韦格勒、埃莱奥诺雷和贝多芬彼此的书信中可以看到的。当三个人到了老年的时候，情爱格外动人，而心灵的年轻却又不减当年。[①]他的老师内夫（C. G. Neefe, 1748—1798）也是他最好的朋友和指导：他的道德的高尚和艺术胸襟的宽广，都对贝多芬产生了极其重要的影响。

贝多芬的童年尽管如是悲惨，他对这个时代和消磨这时代的地方，却永远保持着一种温柔而凄凉的回忆。不得不离开波恩，几乎终身都住在轻佻的都城维也纳及其惨淡的近郊，他却从没忘记莱茵河畔的故乡，庄严的父性的大河，像他所称的"我们的父亲莱茵"；的确，它是那样的生动，几乎赋有人性似的，仿佛一颗巨大的灵魂，无数的思想与力量在其中流过；而且莱茵河流域中也没有一个地方比细腻的波恩更美，更雄壮，更温柔的了，它的浓荫密布、鲜花满地的坂坡，受着河流的冲击与抚爱。在此，贝

---

① 他们的书信，读者可参看本书《书信集》。

多芬消磨了他最初的二十年；在此，形成了他少年心中的梦境，——慵懒地拂着水面的草原上，雾氛笼罩着的白杨，丛密的矮树，细柳和果树，把根须浸在静寂而湍急的水流里，——还有是村落、教堂、墓园，懒洋洋地睁着好奇的眼睛俯视两岸，——远远地，蓝色的七峰在天空画出严峻的侧影，上面矗立着废圮的古堡，显出一些瘦削而古怪的轮廓。他的心对于这个乡土是永久忠诚的；直到生命的终了，他老是想再见故园一面而不能如愿。"我的家乡，我出生的美丽的地方，在我眼前始终是那样的美，那样的明亮，和我离开它时毫无两样。"①

大革命爆发了，泛滥全欧，占据了贝多芬的心。波恩大学是新思想的集中点。1789 年 5 月 14 日，贝多芬报名入学，听有名的厄洛热·施奈德讲德国文学，——他是未来的下莱茵州的检察官。当波恩得悉巴士底狱攻陷时，施奈德在讲坛上朗诵了一首慷慨激昂的诗，②鼓起了学生们如醉如狂的热情。次年，他又印行了一部革命诗集。③在预约者的名单中，④我们可以看到贝多芬和布罗伊宁的

---

① 以上见 1801 年 6 月 29 日致韦格勒书。

② 诗的开首是："专制的铁链斩断了 …… 幸福的民族！……"

③ 我们可举其中一首为例："唾弃偏执，摧毁愚蠢的幽灵，为着人类而战斗……啊，这，没有一个亲王的臣仆能够干。这，需要自由的灵魂，爱死甚于爱谄媚，爱贫穷甚于爱奴颜婢膝……须知在这等灵魂内我绝非最后一个。"
译注：施奈德生于巴伐利亚邦，为斯特拉斯堡雅各宾党首领。1794 年，在巴黎上断头台。

④ 译注：从前著作付印时必先售预约。因印数不多，刊行后不易购得。

名字。

1792 年 11 月，正当战事①蔓延到波恩时，贝多芬离开了故乡，住到德意志的音乐首都维也纳去。②路上他遇见开向法国的黑森军队。③无疑地，他受着爱国情绪的鼓动，在 1796 与 1797 年两年内，他把弗里贝格的战争诗谱成音乐：一阕是《行军曲》，一阕是《我们是伟大的德意志族》。但他尽管讴歌大革命的敌人也是徒然：大革命已征服了世界，征服了贝多芬。从 1798 年起，虽然奥国和法国的关系很紧张，贝多芬仍和法国人有亲密的往还，和使馆方面，和才到维也纳的贝尔纳多德。④在那些谈话里，他的拥护共和的情绪愈益肯定，在他以后的生活中，我们更可看到这股情绪的有力的发展。

这时代施泰因豪泽替他画的肖像，把他当时的面目表现得相当准确。这一幅像之于贝多芬以后的肖像，无异介朗的拿破仑肖像⑤之于别的拿破仑像，那张严峻的脸，活

---

① 译注：此系指法国大革命后奥国为援助法国王室所发动之战争。

② 1787 年春，他曾到维也纳做过一次短期旅行，见过莫扎特，但对方对贝多芬似乎不甚注意。——他于 1790 年在波恩结识的海顿，曾经教过他一些功课。贝多芬另外曾拜过阿尔布雷希茨贝格（J. G. Albrechtsberger，1736—1809）与萨列里（Antonio Salieri，1750—1825）为师。

③ 译注：黑森为当时日耳曼三联邦之一，后皆并入德意志联邦。

④ 在贝氏周围，还有提琴家鲁道夫·克勒策（Rodolphe Kreutzer，1766—1831），后来即贝多芬把有名的奏鸣曲题赠给他。

译注：贝氏为法国元帅，在大革命时以战功显；后与拿破仑为敌，与英、奥诸国勾结。

⑤ 译注：介朗（Pierre-Narcisse Guérin，1774—1833）为法国名画家，所作拿破仑像代表拿翁少年时期之姿态。

现出波拿巴充满着野心的火焰。贝多芬在画上显得很年轻，似乎不到他的年纪，瘦削的，笔直的，高领使他头颈僵直，一副睥睨一切和紧张的目光。他知道他的意志所在；他相信自己的力量。1796年，他在笔记簿上写道："勇敢啊！虽然身体不行，我的天才终究会获胜……二十五岁！不是已经临到了吗？……就在这一年上，整个的人应当显示出来了。"[①]特·伯恩哈德夫人和葛林克说他很高傲，举止粗野，态度抑郁，带着非常强烈的内地口音。但他藏在这骄傲的笨拙之下的慈悲，唯有几个亲密的朋友知道。他写信给韦格勒叙述他的成功时，第一个念头是："譬如我看见一个朋友陷于窘境：倘若我的钱袋不够帮助他时，我只消坐在书桌前面；顷刻之间便解决了他的困难……你瞧这多美妙。"[②]随后他又道："我的艺术应当使可怜的人得益。"

然而痛苦已在叩门；它一朝住在他身上之后永远不再退隐。1796年至1800年，耳聋已开始它的酷刑。[③]耳朵

---

① 那时他才初露头角，在维也纳的首次钢琴演奏会是1795年3月30日举行的。

② 以上见1801年6月29日致韦格勒书。1801年左右致里斯书中又言："只要我有办法，我的任何朋友都不该有何匮乏。"

③ 在1802年的遗嘱内，贝多芬说耳聋已开始了六年——所以是1796年起的。同时我们可注意他的作品目录，唯有包括三支三重奏的作品第一号，是1796年以前的制作。包括三支最初的奏鸣曲的作品第二号，是1796年3月刊行的。因此贝多芬几乎全部的作品可说都是耳聋后写的。关于他的耳聋，可以参看1905年5月15日德国《医学丛报》上克洛－福雷斯脱医生的文章。他认为这病是受一般遗传的影响，也许跟他母亲的肺病也有关系。他分析贝多芬1796年所患的耳咽管炎，到1799年变成剧烈的中耳炎，因为治疗不善，随后成为慢性的中耳炎，随带一切的后果。耳聋的程度逐渐增加，但从没完 （转第12页）

大约 30 岁的贝多芬
卡尔·特劳戈特·里德创作，1801 年

日夜作响；他内脏也受剧烈的痛楚磨折。听觉越来越衰退。在好几年中他瞒着人家，连对最心爱的朋友们也不说；他避免与人见面，使他的残废不致被人发现；他独自守着这可怕的秘密。但到1801年，他不能再缄默了；他绝望地告诉两个朋友——韦格勒医生和阿门达牧师：

"我的亲爱的、我的善良的、我的恳挚的阿门达……我多希望你能常在我身旁！你的贝多芬真是可怜已极。得知道我的最高贵的一部分，我的听觉，大大地衰退了。当我们同在一起时，我已觉得许多病象，我瞒着；但从此越来越恶劣……还会痊愈吗？我当然如此希望，可是非常渺茫；这一类的病是无药可治的。我得过着凄凉的生活，避免我心爱的一切人物，尤其是在这个如此可怜、如此自私的世界上！……我不得不在伤心的隐忍中找栖身！固然我曾发誓要超临这些祸害；但又如何可能？……"[①]

他写信给韦格勒时说："我过着一种悲惨的生活。两年以来我躲避着一切交际，因为我不可能与人说话：我聋了。要是我干着别的职业，也许还可以；但在我的行当里，这是可怕的遭遇啊。我的敌人们又将怎么说？他们的数目又是相当可观！……在戏院里，我得坐在贴近乐队的地

（接第10页）全聋。贝多芬对于低而深的音比高音更易感知。在他晚年，据说他用一支小木杆，一端插在钢琴箱内，一端咬在牙齿中间，用以在作曲时听音。1910年，柏林—莫皮特市立医院主任医师雅各布松发表一篇出色的文章，说他可证明贝多芬的耳聋是源于梅毒的遗传。1814年左右，机械家梅尔策尔为贝多芬特制的听音器，至今尚保存于波恩城内贝多芬博物院。

① 以上见诺尔编《贝多芬书信集》第十三。

方，才能懂得演员的说话。我听不见乐器和歌唱的声音，假如我的座位稍远的话……人家柔和地说话时，我勉强听到一些；人家高声叫喊时，我简直痛苦难忍……我时常诅咒我的生命……普卢塔克①教我学习隐忍。我却愿和我的命运挑战，只要可能；但有些时候，我竟是上帝最可怜的造物……隐忍！多伤心的避难所！然而这是我唯一的出路！"②

这种悲剧式的愁苦，在当时一部分的作品里有所表现，例如作品第十三号的《悲怆奏鸣曲》（1799），尤其是作品第十号（1798）之三的奏鸣曲中的 Largo（广板）。奇怪的是并非所有的作品都带忧郁的情绪，还有许多乐曲，如欢悦的《七重奏》（1800），明澈如水的《第一交响曲》（C 大调，1800）都反映着一种青年人的天真。无疑地，要使心灵惯于愁苦也得相当的时间。它是那样地需要欢乐，当它实际没有欢乐时就自己来创造。当"现在"太残酷时，它就在"过去"中生活。往昔美妙的岁月，一下子是消灭不了的；它们不复存在时，光芒还会悠久地照耀。独自一人在维也纳遭难的辰光，贝多芬便隐遁在故园的忆念里；那时代他的思想都印着这种痕迹。《七重奏》内以变奏曲（Variation）出现的 Andante（行板）的主题，便是一支莱茵的歌谣。《第一交响曲》也是一件颂赞莱茵的作品，是青年人对着梦境微笑的诗歌。它是快乐的，慵懒的；其中有取悦于人的欲念和希望。但在某些段落内，在引子

---

① 译注：系纪元一世纪时希腊伦理学家与史家。

② 以上见《贝多芬书信集》第十四。

（Introduction）里，在低音乐器的明暗的对照里，在神圣的 Scherzo（谐谑曲）里，我们何等感动地，在青春的脸上看到未来的天才的目光。那是波提切利①在《圣家庭》中所画的幼婴的眼睛，其中已可窥到他未来的悲剧。②

　　在这些肉体的痛苦之上，再加另外一种痛苦。韦格勒说他从没见过贝多芬不抱着一股剧烈的热情。这些爱情似乎永远是非常纯洁的。热情与欢娱之间毫无连带关系。现代的人们把这两者混为一谈，实在是他们全不知道何谓热情，也不知道热情之如何难得。贝多芬的心灵里多少有些清教徒气息；粗野的谈吐与思想，他是厌恶的：他对于爱情的神圣抱着毫无假借的观念。据说他不能原谅莫扎特，因为他不惜屈辱自己的天才去写《唐·璜》。③他的密友申德勒确言，"他一生保着童贞，从未有何缺德需要忏悔"。这样的一个人是生来受爱情的欺骗，做爱情的牺牲品的。他的确如此。他不断地钟情，如醉如狂般颠倒，他不断地梦想着幸福，然而立刻幻灭，随后是悲苦的煎熬。贝多芬最丰满的灵感，就当在这种时而热爱、时而骄傲地反抗的轮回中去探寻根源；直到相当的年龄，他的激昂的性格，才在凄恻的隐忍中趋于平静。

　　1801 年时，他热情的对象是朱丽埃塔·圭恰迪妮，为他题赠那著名的作品第二十七号之二的《月光奏鸣曲》

---

① 译注：系文艺复兴前期意大利名画家。

② 译注：此处所谓幼婴系指儿时的耶稣，故有"未来的悲剧"之喻。

③ 译注：唐·璜为西洋传说中有名的登徒子，莫扎特曾采为歌剧的题材。

（1802），而知名于世的。①他写信给韦格勒说："现在我生活比较甜美，和人家来往也较多了些……这变化是一个亲爱的姑娘的魅力促成的；她爱我，我也爱她。这是两年来我初次遇到的幸运的日子。"②可是他为此付了很高的代价。第一，这段爱情使他格外感到自己的残疾，境况的艰难，使他无法娶他所爱的人。其次，圭恰迪妮是风骚的，稚气的，自私的，使贝多芬苦恼；1803 年 11 月，她嫁了加伦贝格伯爵。③——这样的热情是摧残心灵的；而像贝多芬那样，心灵已因疾病而变得虚弱的时候，狂乱的情绪更有把它完全毁灭的危险。他一生就只是这一次，似乎到了颠蹶的关头。他经历着一个绝望的苦闷时期，只消读他那时写给兄弟卡尔与约翰的遗嘱便可知道，遗嘱上注明"等我死后开拆"。④这是惨痛之极的呼声，也是反抗的呼声。我们听着不由不充满着怜悯，他差不多要结束他的生命了。就只靠着他坚强的道德情操才把他止住。⑤他对病愈的最后的

---

① 译注：通俗音乐书上所述《月光奏鸣曲》的故事是毫无根据的。

② 以上见 1801 年 11 月 16 日信。

③ 随后她还利用贝多芬以前的情爱，要他帮助她的丈夫。贝多芬立刻答应了。他在 1821 年和申德勒会见时在谈话手册上写道："他是我的敌人，所以我更要尽力帮助他。"但他因之而更瞧不起她。"她到维也纳来找我，一边哭着，但是我瞧不起她。"

④ 时为 1802 年 10 月 6 日。参见本书《贝多芬遗嘱》。

⑤ 他的遗嘱里有一段说："把德行教给你们的孩子；使人幸福的是德行而非金钱。这是我的经验之谈。在患难中支持我的是道德，使我不曾自杀的，除了艺术以外也是道德。"又 1810 年 5 月 2 日致韦格勒书中："假如我不知道一个人在能完成善的行为时就不该结束生命的话，我早已不在人世了，而且是由于我自己的处决。"

希望没有了。"连一向支持我的卓绝的勇气也消失了。噢，神！给我一天真正的欢乐吧，就是一天也好！我没有听到欢乐的深远的声音已经多久！什么时候，噢！我的上帝，什么时候我再能和它相遇？……永远不？——不？——不，这太残酷了！"

这是临终的哀诉；可是贝多芬还活了二十五年。他的强毅的天性不能遇到磨难就屈服。"我的体力和智力突飞猛进……我的青春，是的，我感到我的青春不过才开始。我窥见我不能加以肯定的目标，我每天都迫近它一些……噢！如果我摆脱了这疾病，我将拥抱世界！……一些休息都没有！除了睡眠以外我不知还有什么休息；而可怜我对于睡眠不得不花费比以前更多的时间。但愿我能在疾病中解放出一半：那时候！……不，我受不了。我要扼住命运的咽喉。它决不能使我完全屈服……噢！能把人生活上千百次，真是多美！"①

这爱情，这痛苦，这意志，这时而颓丧时而骄傲的转换，这些内心的悲剧，都反映在 1802 年的大作品里：附有葬礼进行曲的奏鸣曲（作品第二十六号）；俗称为《月光曲》的《幻想奏鸣曲》（作品第二十七号之二）；作品第三十一号之二的奏鸣曲，——其中戏剧式的吟诵体恍如一场伟大而凄婉的独白；题献亚历山大皇的提琴奏鸣曲（作品第三十号）；《克勒策奏鸣曲》（作品第四十七号）；依着格勒

———————

① 以上见致韦格勒书，《贝多芬书信集》第十八。

特[①]的词句所谱的六支悲壮惨痛的宗教歌（作品第四十八号）；至于1803年的《第二交响曲》，却反映着他年少气盛的情爱；显然是他的意志占了优势。一种无可抵抗的力把忧郁的思想一扫而空。生命的沸腾掀起了乐曲的终局。贝多芬渴望幸福；不肯相信他无可救药的灾难；他渴望痊愈，渴望爱情，他充满着希望。[②]

这些作品里有好几部，进行曲和战斗的节奏特别强烈。这在《第二交响曲》的Allegro（快板）与终局内已很显著，但尤其是献给亚历山大皇的奏鸣曲的第一章，更富于英武壮烈的气概。这种音乐所特有的战斗性，令人想起产生它的时代。大革命已经到了维也纳。[③]贝多芬被它煽动了。骑士赛弗里德说："他在亲密的友人中间，很高兴地谈论政局，用着非常的聪明下判断，目光犀利而且明确。"他所有的同情都倾向于革命党人。在他生命晚期最熟知他的申德勒说："他爱共和的原则。他主张无限制的自由与民族的独立……他渴望大家协力同心地建立

---

① 译注：格勒特（Christian Fürchtegott Gellert，1715—1769），德国启蒙运动作家和诗人。

② 1802年赫内曼为贝多芬所作之小像上，他作着当时流行的装束，留着鬓角，四周的头发剪得同样长，坚决的神情颇像拜伦式的英雄，同时表示一种拿破仑式的永不屈服的意志。

译注：此处小像系指面积极小之釉绘像，通常至大不过数英寸，多数画于珐琅质之饰物上，为西洋画中一种特殊的肖像画。

③ 译注：拿破仑于1793、1797、1800年数次战败奥国，兵临维也纳城下。

国家的政府①……渴望法国实现普选，希望波拿巴建立起这个制度来，替人类的幸福奠定基石。"他仿佛一个革命的古罗马人，受着普卢塔克的熏陶，梦想着一个英雄的共和国，由胜利之神建立的：而所谓胜利之神便是法国的首席执政；于是他接连写下《英雄交响曲：波拿巴》②（1804），帝国的史诗；和《第五交响曲》（1805—1808）的终局，光荣的叙事歌。第一阕真正革命的音乐：时代之魂在其中复活了，那么强烈，那么纯洁，因为当代巨大的变故在孤独的巨人心中是显得强烈与纯洁的，这种印象即和现实接触之下也不会减损分毫。贝多芬的面目，似乎都受着这些历史战争的反映。在当时的作品里，到处都有它们的踪影，也许作者自己不曾觉察，在《科里奥

---

① 译注：意谓共和民主的政府。

② 大家知道《英雄交响曲》是以波拿巴为题材而献给他的。最初的手稿上还写着"波拿巴"这题目。这期间，他得悉了拿破仑称帝之事。于是他大发雷霆，嚷道："那么他也不过是一个凡夫俗子！"愤慨之下，他撕去了题献的词句，换上一个含有报复意味而又是非常动人的题目："英雄交响曲……纪念一个伟大的遗迹"。申德勒说他以后对拿破仑的恼恨也消解了，只把他看作一个值得同情的可怜虫，一个从天上掉下来的"伊加"。（译注：神话载伊加用蜡把翅翼胶住在身上，从克里特岛上逃出，飞近太阳，蜡为日光熔化，以致堕海而死。）当他在1821年听到幽禁圣赫勒拿岛的悲剧时，说道："十七年前我所写的音乐正适用于这件悲惨的事故。"他很高兴地发觉在交响曲的葬曲内（译注：系交响曲之第二章）对此盖世豪雄的结局有所预感。——因此很可能，在贝多芬的思想内，第三交响曲，尤其是第一章，是波拿巴的一幅肖像，当然和实在的人物不同，但确是贝多芬理想中的拿破仑；换言之，他要把拿破仑描写为一个革命的天才。1801年，贝多芬曾为标准的革命英雄，自由之神普罗米修斯，作过乐曲，其中有一主句，他又在《英雄交响曲》的终局里重新采用。

兰序曲》（1807）内，有狂风暴雨在呼啸；《第四四重奏》（作品第十八号）的第一章，和上述的序曲非常相似；《热情奏鸣曲》（作品第五十七号，1804），俾斯麦曾经说过："倘我常听到它，我的勇气将永远不竭。"[①]还有《哀格蒙特序曲》；甚至《降E大调钢琴协奏曲》（作品第七十三号，1809），其中炫耀技巧的部分都是壮烈的，仿佛有人马奔突之势。——而这也不足为怪。在贝多芬写作品第二十六号奏鸣曲中的"英雄葬曲"时，比《英雄交响曲》的主人翁更配他讴歌的英雄，霍赫将军，正战死在莱茵河畔，他的纪念像至今屹立在科布伦茨与波恩之间的山岗上，——即使当时贝多芬不曾知道这件事，他在维也纳也已目击两次革命的胜利。[②]1805年11月，当《菲岱里奥》[③]初次上演时，在座的便有法国军佐。于兰将军，巴士底狱的胜利者，住在洛布科维兹[④]家里，做着贝多芬的朋友兼保护人，受着他《英雄交响曲》与《第五交响曲》

---

① 曾任德国驻意大使的罗伯特·特·科伊德尔，著有《俾斯麦及其家庭》一书，1901版。以上事实均引自该书。1870年10月30日，科伊德尔在凡尔赛的一架很坏的钢琴上，为俾斯麦奏这支奏鸣曲。对于这件作品的最后一句，俾斯麦说："这是整整一个人生的斗争与嚎恸。"他爱贝多芬甚于一切旁的音乐家，他常常说："贝多芬最适合我的神经。"

② 译注：拿破仑曾攻陷维也纳两次。——霍赫为法国大革命时最纯洁的军人，为史所称。1797年战死在科布伦茨附近。

③ 贝多芬的歌剧。

④ 洛氏为波希米亚世家，以武功称。

的题赠。1809 年 5 月 10 日，拿破仑驻节在舍恩布伦。[①]
不久贝多芬便厌恶法国的征略者。但他对于法国人史诗般
的狂热，依旧很清楚地感觉到；所以凡是不能像他那样感
觉的人，对于他这种行动与胜利的音乐决不能彻底了解。

贝多芬突然中止了他的《第五交响曲》，不经过惯有
的拟稿手续，一口气写下了《第四交响曲》。幸福在他眼
前显现了。1806 年 5 月，他和特雷泽·冯·布伦瑞克订了
婚。[②]她老早就爱上他。从贝多芬卜居维也纳的初期，和
她的哥哥弗朗索瓦伯爵为友，她还是一个小姑娘，跟着贝
多芬学钢琴时起，就爱他的。1806 年，他在他们匈牙利的
马尔托伐萨家里作客，在那里他们才相爱起来。关于这些
幸福的日子的回忆，还保存在特雷泽·冯·布伦瑞克的一

---

① 贝多芬的寓所离维也纳的城堡颇近，拿破仑攻下维也纳时曾炸
毁城垣。1809 年 6 月 26 日，贝多芬致布赖特科普夫与埃泰尔两出
版家书信中有言："何等野蛮的生活，在我周围多少的废墟颓垣！只
有鼓声、喇叭声，以及各种惨象！"1809 年有一个法国人在维也纳
见到他，保留着他的一幅肖像。这位法国人叫作特雷蒙男爵。他曾
描写贝多芬寓所中凌乱的情形。他们一同谈论着哲学、政治，特别
是"他的偶像，莎士比亚"。贝多芬几乎决定跟男爵上巴黎去，他知
道那边的音乐院已在演奏他的交响曲，并且有不少佩服他的人。
译注：舍恩布伦为奥国一乡村，1809 年的维也纳条约，即在此处签订。
② 1796 至 1799 年间，贝多芬在维也纳认识了布伦瑞克一家。朱丽
埃塔·圭恰迪妮是特雷泽的表姊妹。贝多芬有一个时期似乎也钟情
于特雷泽的姊妹约瑟菲娜，她后来嫁给戴姆伯爵，又再嫁给施塔克
尔贝格男爵。关于布伦瑞克一家的详细情形，可参看安德烈·特·海
来西氏著《贝多芬及其不朽的爱人》一文，载于 1910 年 3 月 1 日及
15 日的《巴黎杂志》。

34 岁的贝多芬

维利布罗德·约瑟夫·梅勒创作，1804 年

部分叙述里。她说："一个星期日的晚上，用过了晚餐，在月光下贝多芬坐在钢琴前面。先是他放平着手指在键盘上来回抚弄。我和弗朗索瓦都知道他这种习惯。他往往是这样开场的。随后他在低音部分奏了几个和弦；接着，慢慢地，他用一种神秘的庄严的神气，奏着赛巴斯蒂安·巴赫的一支歌：'若愿素心相赠，无妨悄悄相传；两情脉脉，勿为人知。'①

"母亲和教士②都已就寝；哥哥严肃地凝眸睇视着；我的心已被他的歌和目光渗透了，感到生命的丰满。——次日早上，我们在园中相遇。他对我说：'我正在写一本歌剧。主要的人物在我心中，在我面前，不论我到什么地方，停留在什么地方，他总和我同在。我从没到过这般崇高的境界。一切都是光明和纯洁。在此以前，我只像童话里的孩子，只管捡取石子，而不看见路上美艳的鲜花……'1806 年 5 月，只获得我最亲爱的哥哥的同意，我和他订了婚。"

这一年所写的《第四交响曲》，是一朵精纯的花，蕴藏着他一生比较平静的日子的香味。人家说："贝多芬那时竭力要把他的天才，和一般人在前辈大师留下的形式中所认识与爱好的东西，加以调和。"③这是不错的。同样渊源于爱情的妥协精神，对他的举动和生活方式也发生了

---

① 这首美丽的歌是在巴赫的夫人安娜·玛格达兰娜的手册上的，原题为《乔瓦尼尼之歌》。有人疑非巴赫原作。

② 译注：欧洲贵族家中，皆有教士供养。

③ 见诺尔著《贝多芬传》。

影响。赛弗里德和格里尔巴策①说他兴致很好，心灵活跃，处世接物彬彬有礼，对可厌的人也肯忍耐，穿着很讲究；而且他巧妙地瞒着大家，甚至令人不觉得他耳聋；他们说他身体很好，除了目光有些近视之外。②在梅勒替他画的肖像上，我们也可看到一种罗曼蒂克的风雅，微微有些不自然的神情。贝多芬要博人欢心，并且知道已经博得人家欢心。猛狮在恋爱中：它的利爪藏起来了。但在他的眼睛深处，甚至在《第四交响曲》的幻梦与温柔的情调之下，我们仍能感到那可怕的力，任性的脾气，突发的愤怒。

这种深邃的和平并不持久；但爱情的美好的影响一直保存到1810年。无疑是靠了这个影响贝多芬才获得自主力，这使他的天才产生了最完满的果实，例如那古典的悲剧：《第五交响曲》；——那夏日的神明的梦：《田园交响曲》（1808）。③还有他自认为他奏鸣曲中最有力的，从莎士比亚的《暴风雨》感悟得来的《热情奏鸣曲》（1807），为他题献给特雷泽的。④作品第七十八号的富于幻梦与神秘气

---

① 译注：赛弗里德（Ignaz Von Seyfried，1776—1841）系奥地利音乐家；格里尔巴策（Franz Grillparzer，1791—1872）为奥地利剧作家。

② 贝多芬是近视眼。赛弗里德说他的近视是痘症所致，使他从小就得戴眼镜。近视使他的目光常有失神的样子。1823—1824年间，他在书信中常抱怨他的眼睛使他受苦。

③ 把歌德的剧本《哀格蒙特》谱成音乐是1809年开始的。他也想制作《威廉·退尔》的音乐，但人家宁可请教别的作曲家。

④ 见贝多芬和申德勒的谈话。申德勒问贝多芬："你的D小调奏鸣曲和F小调奏鸣曲的内容究竟是什么？"贝多芬答道："请你读读莎士比亚的《暴风雨》去吧！"贝多芬《第十七钢琴奏鸣曲》（D小调，作品第三十一号之二）的别名《暴风雨奏鸣曲》即由此来。（转下页）

息的奏鸣曲（1809），也是献给特雷泽的。写给"不朽的爱人"的一封没有日期的信，所表现的他的爱情的热烈，也不下于《热情奏鸣曲》：

　　我的天使，我的一切，我的我……我心头装满了和你说不尽的话……啊！不论我在哪里，你总和我同在……当我想到你星期日以前不曾接到我初次的消息时，我哭了。——我爱你，像你的爱我一样，但还要强得多……啊！天哪！——没有了你是怎样的生活啊！——咫尺，天涯。————……我的不朽的爱人，我的思念一齐奔向你，有时是快乐的，随后是悲哀的，问着命运，问它是否还有接受我们的愿望的一天。——我只能同你在一起过活，否则我就活不了……永远无人再能占有我的心。永远！——永远！——噢，上帝！为何人们相爱时要分离呢？可是我现在的生活是忧苦的生活。你的爱使我同时成为最幸福和最苦恼的人。——安静吧……安静——爱我呀！——今天，——昨天，——多少热烈的憧憬，多少的眼泪对你，——你，——你，——我的生命！——我的一切！别了！——噢！继续爱我呀，——永勿误解你亲爱的 L 的心。——永久是你的——

（接上页）《第二十三钢琴奏鸣曲》（F 小调，作品第五十七号）的别名《热情奏鸣曲》，是出版家克兰兹所加，这首奏鸣曲创作于 1804 至 1805 年，1807 年出版。

永久是我的——永远是我们的。①

什么神秘的理由，阻挠着这一对相爱的人的幸福？——也许是没有财产，地位的不同。也许贝多芬对人家要他长时期的等待，要他把这段爱情保守秘密，感到屈辱而表示反抗。

也许以他暴烈、多病、愤世嫉俗的性情，无形中使他的爱人受难，而他自己又因之感到绝望。——婚约毁了；然而两人中间似乎没有一个忘却这段爱情。直到她生命的最后一刻，特雷泽·冯·布伦瑞克还爱着贝多芬。②

1816年时贝多芬说："当我想到她时，我的心仍和第一天见到她时跳得一样的剧烈。"同年，他制作六阕《献给遥远的爱人》的歌。他在笔记内写道："我一见到这个美妙的造物，我的心情就泛滥起来，可是她并不在此，并不在我旁边！"——特雷泽曾把她的肖像赠予贝多芬，题着："给稀有的天才，伟大的艺术家，善良的人。T. B."③在贝多芬晚年，一位朋友无意中撞见他独自拥抱着这幅肖像，哭着，高声地自言自语着（这是他的习惯）："你这样的美，这样的伟大，和天使一样！"朋友退了出去，过了一会再进去，看见他在弹琴，便对他说："今天，我的朋友，你的脸上全无可怕的气色。"贝多芬答道："因为我的好天使来访问过我了。"——创伤深深地铭刻在他心上。他自

---

① 见《贝多芬书信集》第十五。
② 她死于1861年。译注：她比贝多芬多活三十四年。
③ 这幅肖像至今还在波恩的贝多芬家。

己说："可怜的贝多芬，此世没有你的幸福。只有在理想的境界里才能找到你的朋友。"①

他在笔记上又写着："屈服，深深地向你的运命屈服：你不复能为你自己而存在，只能为着旁人而存在；为你，只在你的艺术里才有幸福。噢，上帝！给我勇气让我征服我自己！"

爱情把他遗弃了。1810 年，他重又变成孤独；但光荣已经来到，他也显然感到自己的威力。他正当盛年。②他完全放纵他的暴烈与粗犷的性情，对于社会，对于习俗，对于旁人的意见，对一切都不顾虑。他还有什么需要畏惧，需要敷衍？爱情，没有了；野心，没有了。所剩下的只有力，力的欢乐，需要应用它，甚至滥用它。"力，这才是和寻常人不同的人的精神！"他重复不修边幅，举止也愈加放肆。他知道他有权可以言所欲言，即对世间最大的人物亦然如此。"除了仁慈以外，我不承认还有什么优越的标记"，这是他 1812 年 7 月 17 日所写的话。③贝蒂娜·布伦塔诺④那时看见他，说"没有一个皇帝对于自己的力有他这样坚

<hr>

① 致格莱兴施泰因书。《贝多芬书信集》第三十一。

② 译注：贝多芬此时四十岁。

③ 他写给 G. D. 里奥的信中又道："心是一切伟大的起点。"《贝多芬书信集》一〇八。

④ 译注：贝系歌德的青年女友，贝母曾与歌德相爱；故贝成年后竭力追求歌德。贝对贝多芬备极崇拜，且对贝多芬音乐极有了解。贝兄克莱门斯（1778—1892）为德国浪漫派领袖之一。贝丈夫阿宁亦为有名诗人。

强的意识"。她被他的威力慑服了，写信给歌德时说道："当我初次看见他时，整个世界在我面前消失了，贝多芬使我忘记了世界，甚至忘记了你，噢，歌德！……我敢断言这个人物远远地走在现代文明之前，而我相信我这句话是不错的。"①

歌德设法要认识贝多芬。1812年，终于他们在波希米亚的浴场特普利兹地方相遇，结果却不很投机。贝多芬热烈佩服着歌德的天才；②但他过于自由和过于暴烈的性格，不能和歌德的性格融和，而不免于伤害他。他曾叙述他们一同散步的情景，当时这位骄傲的共和党人，把魏玛大公的枢密参赞③教训了一顿，使歌德永远不能原谅。

君王与公卿尽可造成教授与机要参赞，尽可

---

① 译注：贝蒂娜写此信时，约为1808年，尚未满二十九岁。此时贝多芬未满四十岁，歌德年最长，已有六十岁左右。
② 1811年2月19日他写给贝蒂娜的信中说："歌德的诗使我幸福。"1809年8月8日他在旁的书信中也说："歌德与席勒，是我在莪相与荷马之外最心爱的诗人。"——值得注意的是，贝多芬幼年的教育虽不完全，但他的文学口味极高。在他认为"伟大，庄严，D小调式的"歌德以外而看作高于歌德的，只有荷马、普卢塔克、莎士比亚三人。在荷马作品中，他最爱《奥德赛》。莎士比亚的德译本是常在他手头的，我们也知道莎士比亚的《科利奥兰纳斯》和《暴风雨》被他多么悲壮地在音乐上表现出来。至于普卢塔克，他和大革命时代的一般人一样，受有很深的影响。古罗马英雄布鲁图斯是他的英雄，这一点他和米开朗琪罗相似。他爱柏拉图，梦想在全世界上能有柏拉图式的共和国建立起来。1819—1820年间的谈话册内，他曾言："苏格拉底与耶稣是我的模范。"
③ 译注：此系歌德官衔。

赏赐他们头衔与勋章；但他们不能造成伟大的人物，不能造成超临庸俗社会的心灵；……而当像我和歌德这样两个人在一起时，这般君侯贵胄应当感到我们的伟大。——昨天，我们在归路上遇见全体的皇族。①我们远远地就已看见。歌德挣脱了我的手臂，站在大路一旁。我徒然对他说尽我所有的话，不能使他再走一步。于是我按了一按帽子，扣上外衣的钮子，背着手，往最密的人丛中撞去。亲王与近臣密密层层；太子鲁道夫②对我脱帽；皇后先对我招呼。——那些大人先生是认得我的。——为了好玩起计，我看着这队人马在歌德面前经过。他站在路边上，深深地弯着腰，帽子拿在手里。事后我大大地教训了他一顿，毫不同他客气……③

而歌德也没有忘记。④

---

① 译注：系指奥国王室，特普利兹为当时避暑胜地，中欧各国的亲王贵族麇集。

② 译注：系贝多芬的钢琴学生。

③ 以上见贝多芬致贝蒂娜书。这些书信的真实性虽有人怀疑，但大体是准确的。

④ 歌德写信给策尔特说："贝多芬不幸是一个倔强之极的人；他认为世界可憎，无疑是对的；但这并不能使世界对他和对旁人变得愉快些。我们应当原谅他，替他惋惜，因为他是聋子。"歌德一生不曾做什么事反对贝多芬，但也不曾做什么事拥护贝多芬；对他的作品，甚至对他的姓氏，抱着绝对的缄默。骨子里他是钦佩而且惧怕他的（转下页）

《第七交响曲》和《第八交响曲》便是这时代的作品，就是说1812年在特普利兹写的：前者是节奏的大祭乐，后者是诙谐的交响曲，他在这两件作品内也许最是自在，像他自己所说的，最是"尽量"，那种快乐与狂乱的激动，出其不意的对比，使人错愕的夸大的机智，巨人式的、使歌德与策尔特惶骇的爆发，[①]使德国北部流行着一种说数，说《第七交响曲》是一个酒徒的作品。——不错，是一个沉醉的人的作品，但也是力和天才的产物。

———————

（接上页）音乐：它使他骚乱。他怕它会使他丧失心灵的平衡，那是歌德以多少痛苦换来的。——年轻的门德尔松，于1830年经过魏玛，曾经留下一封信，表示他确曾参透歌德自称为"骚乱而热烈的灵魂"深处，那颗灵魂是被歌德用强有力的智慧镇压着的。门德尔松在信中说："……他先是不愿听人提及贝多芬；但这是无可避免的（译注：门德尔松那次是奉歌德之命替他弹全部音乐史上的大作品），他听了《第五交响曲》的第一章后大为骚动。他竭力装作镇静，和我说：'这毫不动人，不过令人惊异而已。'过了一会儿，他又道：'这是巨大的，——译注：歌德原词是Grandiose，含有伟大或夸大的模棱两可的意义，令人猜不透他这里到底是颂赞（假如他的意思是"伟大"的话）还是贬抑（假如他的意思是"夸大"的话）——狂妄的，竟可说屋宇为之震动。'接着是晚膳，其间他神思恍惚，若有所思，直到我们再提起贝多芬时，他开始询问我，考问我。我明明看到贝多芬的音乐已经发生了效果……"

译注：策尔特为一平庸的音乐家，早年反对贝多芬甚烈，直到后来他遇见贝多芬时，被他的人格大为感动，对他的音乐也一变往昔的谩骂口吻，转而为热烈的颂扬。策氏为歌德一生挚友，歌德早期对贝多芬的印象，大半受策氏误解之影响，关于贝多芬与歌德近人颇多撰文讨论。罗曼·罗兰亦有《歌德与贝多芬》一书，1930版。

[①] 见策尔特1812年9月2日致歌德书，又同年9月14日歌德致策尔特书："是的，我也是用着惊愕的心情钦佩他。"1819年策尔特给歌德信中说："人家说他疯了。"

他自己也说："我是替人类酿制醇醪的酒神。是我给人以精神上至高的热狂。"

瓦格纳说：他不知贝多芬是否想在《第七交响曲》的终局内描写一个酒神的庆祝会。[①]在这阕豪放的乡村节会音乐中，自己特别看到他佛兰芒族的遗传；同样，在以纪律和服从为尚的国家，他的肆无忌惮的举止谈吐，也是渊源于他自身的血统。不论在哪一件作品里，都没有《第七交响曲》那么坦白，那么自由的力。这是无目的地，单为了娱乐而浪费着超人的精力，宛如一条洋溢泛滥的河的欢乐。在《第八交响曲》内，力量固没有这样的夸大，但更加奇特，更表现出作者的特点，交融着悲剧与滑稽，力士般的刚强和儿童般的任性。[②]

1814 年是贝多芬幸运的顶点。在维也纳会议中，人家看他作欧罗巴的光荣。他在庆祝会中非常活跃。亲王们向他致敬，像他自己高傲地向申德勒所说的，他听任他们追逐。

他受着独立战争[③]的鼓动。1813 年，他写了一阕《威灵顿之胜利交响曲》；1814 年初，写了一阕战士的合唱：

---

① 这至少是贝多芬曾经想过的题目，因为他在笔记内曾经说到，尤其他在《第十交响曲》的计划内提及。

② 和写作这些作品同时，他在 1811 至 1812 年间在特普利兹认识一个柏林的青年女歌唱家，和她有着相当温柔的友谊，也许对这些作品不无影响。

③ 在这种事故上和贝多芬大异的，是舒伯特的父亲，在 1807 年时写了一阕应时的音乐《献给拿破仑大帝》，且在拿破仑御前亲自指挥。

译注：拿破仑于 1812 年征俄败归后，1813 年奥国兴师讨法，不久普鲁士亦接踵而起，是即史家所谓独立战争，亦称解放战争。

《德意志的再生》；1814 年 11 月 29 日，他在许多君主前面指挥一支爱国歌曲：《光荣的时节》；1815 年，他为攻陷巴黎①写一首合唱：《大功告成》。这些应时的作品，比他一切旁的音乐更能增加他的声名。布莱修斯·赫弗尔依着弗朗索瓦·勒特龙的素描所作的木刻，和 1813 年弗兰兹·克莱因塑的脸型（Masque），活泼泼地表现出贝多芬在维也纳会议时的面貌。狮子般的脸上，牙床紧咬着，刻画着愤怒与苦恼的皱痕，但表现得最明显的性格是他的意志，早年拿破仑式的意志："可惜我在战争里不像在音乐中那么内行！否则我将战败他！"

但是他的王国不在此世，像他写信给弗朗索瓦·冯·布伦瑞克时所说的："我的王国是在天空。"②

在此光荣的时间以后，接踵而来的是最悲惨的时期。

维也纳从未对贝多芬抱有好感。像他那样一个高傲而独立的天才，在此轻佻浮华、为瓦格纳所痛恶的都城里是不得人心的。③他抓住可以离开维也纳的每个机会；1808

---

① 译注：系指 1814 年 3 月奥德各邦联军攻入巴黎。

② 他在维也纳会议时写信给考卡说："我不和你谈我们的君王和王国，在我看来，思想之国是一切国家中最可爱的：那是此世和彼世的一切王国中的第一个。"

③ 瓦格纳在 1870 年所著的《贝多芬评传》中有言："维也纳，这不就说明了一切？——全部的德国新教痕迹都已消失，连民族的口音也失掉而变成意大利化。德国的精神，德国的态度和风俗，全经意大利与西班牙输入的指南册代为解释……这是一个历史、学术、宗教都被篡改的地方……轻浮的怀疑主义，毁坏而且埋葬了真理之爱，荣誉之爱，自由独立之爱！……"

（转下页）

年，他很想脱离奥国，到威斯特伐利亚王热罗姆·波拿巴的宫廷①里去。但维也纳的音乐泉源是那么丰富，我们也不该抹杀那边常有一班高贵的鉴赏家，感到贝多芬之伟大，不肯使国家蒙受丧失这天才之羞。1809年，维也纳三个富有的贵族：贝多芬的学生鲁道夫太子，洛布科维兹亲王，金斯基亲王，答应致送他四千弗洛令②的年俸，只要他肯留在奥国。他们说："显然一个人只在没有经济烦虑的时候才能整个地献身于艺术，才能产生这些崇高的作品为艺术增光，所以我们决意使路德维希·凡·贝多芬获得物质的保障，避免一切足以妨害他天才发展的阻碍。"

不幸结果与诺言不符。这笔津贴并未付足；不久又完全停止。且从1814年维也纳会议起，维也纳的性格也转变了。社会的目光从艺术移到政治方面，音乐口味被意大利作风破坏了，时尚所趋的是罗西尼，把贝多芬视为迂

（接上页）十九世纪的奥国戏剧诗人格里尔帕策曾说生为奥国人是一桩不幸。十九世纪末住在维也纳的德国大作曲家，都极感苦闷。那时奥国都城的思想全被勃拉姆斯伪善的气息笼罩。布鲁克纳的生活是长时期的受难，雨果·沃尔夫终生奋斗，对维也纳表示极严厉的批评。

译注：布鲁克纳（Anton Bruckner, 1824—1896）与雨果·沃尔夫（Hugo Wolf, 1860—1903）皆为近代德国大音乐家。勃拉姆斯在当时为反动派音乐之代表。

① 热罗姆王愿致送贝多芬终身俸每年六百杜加（译注：每杜加约合九先令），外加旅费津贴一百五十银币，唯一的条件是不时在他面前演奏，并指挥室内音乐会，那些音乐会是历时很短而且不常举行的。贝多芬差不多决定动身了。

译注：热罗姆王为拿破仑之弟，被封为威斯特伐利亚王。

② 译注：弗洛令为奥国银币名，每单位约合一先令又半。

腐。^①贝多芬的朋友和保护人，分散的分散，死亡的死亡：金斯基亲王死于 1812 年，李希诺夫斯基亲王死于 1814 年，洛布科维兹死于 1816 年。受贝多芬题赠作品第五十九号的美丽的四重奏的拉苏莫夫斯基，在 1815 年举办了最后的一次音乐会。同年，贝多芬和童年的朋友，埃莱奥诺雷的哥哥，斯特凡·冯·布罗伊宁失和。^②从此他孤独了。^③在 1816 年的笔记上，他写道："没有朋友，孤零零地在世界上。"

耳朵完全聋了。^④从 1815 年秋天起，他和人们只有笔上的往还。^⑤最早的谈话手册是 1816 年的。^⑥关于 1822

---

① 罗西尼的歌剧《唐克雷迪》足以撼动整个的德国音乐。1816 年时维也纳沙龙里的意见，据鲍恩费尔德的日记所载是："莫扎特和贝多芬是老学究，只有荒谬的上一代赞成他们；但直到罗西尼出现，大家方知何谓旋律。《菲岱里奥》是一堆垃圾，真不懂人们怎会不怕厌烦地去听它。"——贝多芬举行的最后一次钢琴演奏会是 1814 年。

② 同年，贝多芬的兄弟卡尔死。他写信给安东尼·布伦塔诺说："他如此地执着生命，我却如此地愿意舍弃生命。"

③ 此时唯一的朋友，是玛丽亚·冯·埃尔德迪，他和她维持着动人的友谊，但她和他一样有着不治之症，1816 年，她的独子又暴卒。贝多芬题赠给她的作品，有 1809 年作品第七十号的两支三重奏，1815 至 1817 年间作品第一〇二号的两支大提琴奏鸣曲。

④ 丢开耳聋不谈，他的健康也一天不如一天。从 1816 年 10 月起，他患着重伤风。1817 年夏天，医生说他是肺病。1817 至 1818 年间的冬季，他老是为这场所谓的肺病担心着。1820 至 1821 年间他患着剧烈的关节炎。1821 年患黄热病。1823 年又患结膜炎。

⑤ 值得注意的是，同年起他的音乐作风改变了，表示这转折点的是作品第一〇一号的奏鸣曲。

⑥ 贝多芬的谈话册，共有 11000 页的手写稿，今日全部保存于柏林国家图书馆。1923 年诺尔开始印行他 1819 年 3 月至 1820 年 3 月的谈话册，可惜以后未曾续印。

年《菲岱里奥》预奏会的经过，有申德勒的一段惨痛的记述可按。

"贝多芬要求亲自指挥最后一次的预奏……从第一幕的二部唱起，显而易见他全没听见台上的歌唱。他把乐曲的进行延缓很多；当乐队跟着他的指挥棒进行时，台上的歌手自顾自地匆匆向前。结果是全局都紊乱了。经常的，乐队指挥乌姆劳夫不说明什么理由，提议休息一会儿；和歌唱者交换了几句说话之后，大家重新开始。同样的紊乱又发生了。不得不再休息一次。在贝多芬指挥之下，无疑是干不下去的了；但怎样使他懂得呢？没有一个人有心肠对他说：'走吧，可怜虫，你不能指挥了。'贝多芬不安起来，骚动之余，东张西望，想从不同的脸上猜出症结所在；可是大家都默不作声。他突然用命令的口吻呼唤我。我走近时，他把谈话手册授给我，示意我写。我便写着：'恳求您勿再继续，等回去再告诉您理由。'于是他一跃下台；对我嚷道：'快走！'他一口气跑回家里去；进去，一动不动地倒在便榻上，双手捧着他的脸；他这样一直到晚饭时分。用餐时他一言不发，保持着最深刻的痛苦的表情。晚饭以后，当我想告别时，他留着我，表示不愿独自在家。等到我们分手的辰光，他要我陪着去看医生，以耳科出名的……在我和贝多芬的全部交谊中，没有一天可和这十一月里致命的一天相比。他心坎里受了伤，至死不曾忘记这可怕的一幕的印象。"①

---

① 申德勒从1814年起就和贝多芬来往，但到1819以后方始成为他的密友。贝多芬不肯轻易与之结交，最初对他表示高傲轻蔑的态度。

45 岁的贝多芬

费迪南德·瓦尔德米勒创作，1815 年

两年以后，1824年5月7日，他指挥着（或更准确地，像节目单上所注明的"参与指挥事宜"）《合唱交响曲》①时，他全没听见全场一致的喝彩声；他丝毫不曾觉察，直到一个女歌唱演员牵着他的手，让他面对着群众时，他才突然看见全场起立，挥舞着帽子，向他鼓掌。——一个英国游历家罗素，1825年时看见过他弹琴，说当他要表现柔和的时候，琴键不曾发声，在这静寂中看着他情绪激动的神气，脸部和手指都抽搐起来，真是令人感动。

隐遁在自己的内心生活里，和其余的人类隔绝着，②他只有在自然中觅得些许安慰。特雷泽·布伦瑞克说："自然是他唯一的知己。"它成为他的托庇所。1815年时认识他的查理·纳德，说他从未见过一个人像他这样的爱花木，云彩，自然……他似乎靠着自然生活。③贝多芬写道："世界上没有一个人像我这样的爱田野……我爱一株树甚于爱一个人……"在维也纳时，每天他沿着城墙绕一个圈子。在乡间，从黎明到黑夜，他独自在外散步，不戴帽子，冒着太阳，冒着风雨。"全能的上帝！——在森林中我快乐了，——在森林中我快乐了，——每株树都传达着你的声音。——天哪！何等的神奇！——在这些树林里，在这些岗峦上——一片宁谧，供你役使的宁谧。"

---

① 即《第九交响曲》。
② 参看瓦格纳的《贝多芬评传》，对他的耳聋有极美妙的叙述。
③ 他爱好动物，非常怜悯它们。有名的史家弗里梅尔的母亲，说她不由自主地对贝多芬怀有长时期的仇恨，因为贝多芬在她儿时把她要捕捉的蝴蝶用手帕赶开。

他的精神的骚乱在自然中获得了一些苏慰。①他为金钱的烦虑弄得困惫不堪。1818年时他写道："我差不多到了行乞的地步，而我还得装作日常生活并不艰窘的神气。"此外他又说："作品第一〇六号的奏鸣曲是在紧急情况中写的。要以工作来换取面包实在是一件苦事。"施波尔②说他往往不能出门，为了靴子洞穿之故。他对出版商负着重债，而作品又卖不出钱。《D调弥撒曲》发售预约时，只有七个预约者，其中没有一个是音乐家。③他全部美妙的奏鸣曲④——每曲都得花费他三个月的工作——只给他挣了三十至四十杜加。加利钦亲王要他制作的四重奏（作品第一二七、一三〇、一三二号），也许是他作品中最深刻的，仿佛用血泪写成的，结果是一文都不曾拿到。把贝多芬煎熬完的是，日常的窘况，无穷尽的讼案，或是要人家履行津贴的诺言，或是为争取侄儿的监护权，因为他的兄弟卡尔于1815年死于肺病，遗下一个儿子。

他心坎间洋溢着的温情全部灌注在这个孩子身上。这儿又是残酷的痛苦等待着他。仿佛是境遇的好意，特意替他不断地供给并增加苦难，使他的天才不致缺乏营养。——他先是要和他那个不入流品的弟妇争他的小卡尔，他写道：

---

① 他的居处永远不舒服。在维也纳三十五年，他迁居三十次。

② 译注：路德维希·施波尔（Ludwig Spohr，1784—1859），当时德国的提琴家兼作曲家。

③ 贝多芬写信给凯鲁比尼，"为他在同时代的人中最敬重的"。可是凯鲁比尼置之不理。译注：凯氏为意大利人，为法国音乐院长，作曲家，在当时音乐界中极有势力。

④ 译注：贝多芬钢琴奏鸣曲一项，列在全集内的即有三十二首之多。

"噢，我的上帝，我的城墙，我的防卫，我唯一的托庇所！我的心灵深处，你是一览无余的，我使那些和我争夺卡尔的人受苦时，我的苦痛，你是鉴临的。[1]请你听我呀，我不知如何称呼你的神灵！请你接受我热烈的祈求，我是你造物之中最不幸的可怜虫。"

"噢，神哪！救救我吧！你瞧，我被全人类遗弃，因为我不愿和不义妥协！接受我的祈求吧，让我，至少在将来，能和我的卡尔一起过活！……噢，残酷的命运，不可摇撼的命运！不，不，我的苦难永无终了之日！"

然后，这个热烈地被爱的侄子，显得并不配受伯父的信任。贝多芬给他的书信是痛苦的、愤慨的，宛如米开朗琪罗给他的兄弟们的信，但是更天真更动人：

> 我还得再受一次最卑下的无情义的酬报吗？也罢，如果我们之间的关系要破裂，就让它破裂吧！一切公正的人知道这回事以后，都将恨你……如果连系我们的约束使你不堪担受，那么凭着上帝的名字——但愿一切都照着他的意志实现——我把你交给至圣至高的神明了；我已尽了我所有的力量；我敢站在最高的审判之前……[2]
>
> 像你这样娇养坏的孩子，学一学真诚与朴实

---

① 他写信给施特赖谢尔夫人说："我从不报复。当我不得不有所行动来反对旁人时，我只限于自卫，或阻止他们作恶。"

② 见诺尔编《贝多芬书信集》三四三。

决计于你无害；你对我的虚伪的行为，使我的心太痛苦了，难以忘怀……上帝可以作证，我只想跑到千里之外，远离你，远离这可怜的兄弟和这丑恶的家庭……我不能再信任你了。

下面的署名是：

不幸的是：你的父亲——或更好：不是你的父亲。[1]

但宽恕立刻接踵而至：

我亲爱的儿子！——一句话也不必再说，——到我臂抱里来吧，你不会听到一句严厉的说话……我将用同样的爱接待你。如何安排你的前程，我们将友善地一同商量。——我以荣誉为担保，决无责备的言辞！那是毫无用处的。你能期待于我的只有殷勤和最亲切的帮助。——来吧，来到你父亲的忠诚的心上。——来吧，一接到信立刻回家吧。

（在信封上又用法文写着："如果你不来，我定将为你而死。"）[2]

---

[1] 见诺尔编《贝多芬书信集》三一四。
[2] 见诺尔编《贝多芬书信集》三七〇。

他又哀求道：

> 别说谎，永远做我最亲爱的儿子！如果你用
> 虚伪来报答我，像人家使我相信的那样，那真是
> 何等丑恶何等刺耳！……别了，我虽不曾生下你
> 来，但的确抚养过你，而且竭尽所能地培植过你
> 精神的发展，现在我用着有甚于父爱的情爱，从
> 心坎里求你走上善良和正直的唯一的大路。你的
> 忠诚的老父。①

这个并不缺少聪明的侄儿，贝多芬本想把他领上高等
教育的路，然而替他筹划了无数美妙的前程之梦以后，不
得不答应他去习商。但卡尔出入赌场，负了不少债务。

由于一种可悲的怪现象，比人们想象中更为多见的怪
现象，伯父的精神的伟大，对侄儿非但无益，而且有害，
使他恼怒，使他反抗，如他自己所说的："因为伯父要我上
进，所以我变得更下流"；这种可怕的说话，活活显出这
个浪子的灵魂。他甚至在1826年时在自己头上打了一枪。
然而他并没死，倒是贝多芬几乎因之送命：他为这件事情
所受的难堪，永远无法摆脱。②卡尔痊愈了，他自始至终

---

① 以上见《贝多芬书信集》三六二至三六七。另外一封信，是
1819年2月1日的，里面表示贝多芬多么热望把他的侄子造成"一
个于国家有益的公民"。
② 当时看见他的申德勒，说他突然变得像一个七十岁的老人，精
神崩溃，没有力量，没有意志。倘卡尔死了的话，他也要死的了。——
不多几月之后，他果真一病不起。

使伯父受苦，而对于这伯父之死，也未始没有关系；贝多芬临终的时候，他竟没有在场。——几年以前，贝多芬写给侄子的信中说："上帝从没遗弃我。将来终有人来替我阖上眼睛。"——然而替他阖上眼睛的，竟不是他称为"儿子"的人。

在此悲苦的深渊里，贝多芬从事于讴歌欢乐。

这是他毕生的计划。从1793年他在波恩时起就有这个念头。[1]他一生要歌唱欢乐，把这歌唱作为他某一大作品的结局。颂歌的形式，以及放在哪一部作品里这些问题，他踌躇了一生。即在《第九交响曲》内，他也不曾打定主意。直到最后一刻，他还想把欢乐颂歌留下来，放在第十或第十一的交响曲中去。我们应当注意《第九交响曲》的原题，并非今日大家所习用的《合唱交响曲》，而是"以欢乐颂歌的合唱为结局的交响曲"。《第九交响曲》可能而且应该有另外一种结束。1823年7月，贝多芬还想给它一个器乐的结束，这一段结束，他以后用在作品第一三二号的四

①　见1793年1月菲舍尼希致夏洛特·席勒书。席勒的《欢乐颂》是1785年写的。贝多芬所用的主题，先后见于1808作品第八十号的《钢琴、乐队、合唱幻想曲》，及1810依歌德诗谱成的"歌"。——在1812年的笔记内，在《第七交响曲》的拟稿和《麦克白前奏曲》的计划之间，有一段乐稿是采用席勒原词的，其音乐主题，后来用于作品第一一五号的《纳门斯弗尔前奏曲》。——《第九交响曲》内有些乐旨在1815年以前已经出现。定稿中欢乐颂歌的主题和其他部分的曲调，都是1822年写下的，以后再写Trio（中段）部分，然后又写Andante（行板）、Moderato（中板）部分，直到最后才写成Adagio（柔板）。

重奏内。车尔尼和松莱特纳确言，即在演奏过后（1824 年 5 月），贝多芬还未放弃改用器乐结束的意思。

要在一阕交响曲内引进合唱，有极大的技术上的困难，这是可从贝多芬的稿本上看到的，他作过许多试验，想用别种方式，并在这件作品的别的段落引进合唱。在 Adagio（柔板）的第二主题的稿本上，他写道："也许合唱在此可以很适当地开始。"但他不能毅然决然地和他忠诚的乐队分手。他说："当我看见一个乐思的时候，我总是听见乐器的声音，从未听见人声。"所以他把运用歌唱的时间尽量延宕；甚至先把主题交给器乐来奏出，不但终局的吟诵体为然，[1]连"欢乐"的主题亦是如此。

对于这些延缓和踌躇的解释，我们还得更进一步：它们还有更深刻的原因。这个不幸的人永远受着忧患折磨，永远想讴歌"欢乐"之美；然而年复一年，他延宕着这桩事业，因为他老是卷在热情与哀伤的旋涡内。直到生命的最后一日他才完成了心愿，可是完成的时候是何等的伟大！

当欢乐的主题初次出现时，乐队忽然中止；出其不意地一片静默；这使歌唱的开始带着一种神秘与神明的气概。而这是不错的：这个主题的确是一个神明。"欢乐"自天而降，包裹在非现实的宁静中间：它用柔和的气息抚慰着痛苦；而它溜滑到大病初愈的人的心坎中时，第一下的抚摩又是那么温柔，令人如贝多芬的那个朋友一样，禁不住因

———————————

[1]　贝多芬说这一部分"完全好像有歌词在下面"。

"看到他柔和的眼睛而为之下泪"。当主题接着过渡到人声上去时，先由低音表现，带着一种严肃而受压迫的情调。慢慢地，"欢乐"抓住了生命。这是一种征服，一场对痛苦的斗争。然后是进行曲的节奏，浩浩荡荡的军队，男高音热烈急促的歌，在这些沸腾的乐章内，我们可以听到贝多芬的气息，他的呼吸，与他受着感应的呼喊的节奏，活现出他在田野间奔驰，作着他的乐曲，受着如醉如狂的激情鼓动，宛如大雷雨中的李尔老王。在战争的欢乐之后，是宗教的醉意；随后又是神圣的宴会，又是爱的兴奋。整个的人类向天张着手臂，大声疾呼着扑向"欢乐"，把它紧紧地搂在怀里。

巨人的巨著终于战胜了群众的庸俗。维也纳轻浮的风气，被它震撼了一刹那，这都城当时是完全在罗西尼与意大利歌剧的势力之下的。贝多芬颓丧忧郁之余，正想移居伦敦，到那边去演奏《第九交响曲》。像 1809 年一样，几个高贵的朋友又来求他不要离开祖国。他们说："我们知道您完成了一部新的圣乐，①表现着您深邃的信心感应给您的情操。渗透着您的心灵的超现实的光明，照耀着这件作品。我们也知道您的伟大的交响曲的王冠上，又添了一朵不朽的鲜花……您近几年来的沉默，使一切关注您的人为之凄然。②大家都悲哀地想到，正当外国音乐移植到

---

① 系指《D 调弥撒曲》。

② 贝多芬为琐碎的烦恼、贫穷，以及各种的忧患所困，在 1816 至 1821 的五年中间，只写了三支钢琴曲（作品第一〇一、一〇二、一〇六号）。他的敌人说他才力已尽。1821 年起他才重新工作。

50 岁的贝多芬
约瑟夫·卡尔·斯泰勒创作，1820 年

我们的土地上，令人遗忘德国艺术的产物之时，我们的天才，在人类中占有那么崇高的地位的，竟默无一言……唯有在您身上，整个的民族期待着新生命，新光荣，不顾时下的风气而建立起真与美的新时代……但愿您能使我们的希望不久即实现……但愿靠了您的天才，将来的春天，对于我们，对于人类，加倍的繁荣！"[①]这封慷慨陈词的信，证明贝多芬在德国优秀阶级中所享有的声威，不但是艺术方面的，而且是道德方面的。他的崇拜者称颂他的天才时，所想到的第一个字既非学术，亦非艺术，而是"信仰"。[②]

　　贝多芬被这些言辞感动了，决意留下。1824年5月7日，在维也纳举行《D调弥撒曲》和《第九交响曲》的第一次演奏会，获得空前的成功。情况之热烈，几乎含有暴动的性质。当贝多芬出场时，受到群众五次鼓掌的欢迎；在此讲究礼节的国家，对皇族的出场，习惯也只用三次的鼓掌礼。因此警察不得不出面干涉。交响曲引起狂热的骚动。许多人哭起来。贝多芬在终场以后感动得晕了过去；大家把他抬到申德勒家，他朦朦胧胧地和衣睡着，不饮不食，直到次日早上。可是胜利是暂时的，对贝多芬毫无盈利。音乐会不曾给他挣什么钱。物质生活的窘

---

① 这是1824年的事，署名的有C.李希诺夫斯基亲王等二十余人。

② 1819年2月1日，贝多芬要求对侄子的监护权时，在维也纳市政府高傲地宣称："我的道德的品格是大家公认的。"

迫依然如故。他贫病交迫，^①孤独无依，可是战胜了：^②——战胜了人类的平庸，战胜了他自己的命运，战胜了他的痛苦。

"牺牲，永远把一切人生的愚昧为你的艺术去牺牲！艺术，这是高于一切的上帝！"

因此他已达到了终身想望的目标。他已抓住欢乐。但在这控制着暴风雨的心灵高峰上，他是否能长此逗留？——当然，他还得不时堕入往昔的怆痛里。当然，他最后的几部四重奏里充满着异样的阴影。可是《第九交响曲》的胜利，似乎在贝多芬心中已留下它光荣的标记。他未来的计划^③是:《第十交响曲》^④，《纪念巴赫的前奏曲》，

---

① 1824 年秋，他很担心要在一场暴病中送命。"像我亲爱的祖父一样，我和他有多少地方相似。"他胃病很厉害。1824—1825 间的冬天，他又重病。1825 年 5 月，他吐血，流鼻血。同年 6 月 9 日他写信给侄儿说："我衰弱到了极点，长眠不起的日子快要临到了。"

② 德国首次演奏《第九交响曲》，是 1825 年 4 月 1 日在法兰克福；伦敦是 1825 年 3 月 25 日；巴黎是 1831 年 3 月 27 日，在国立音乐院。十七岁的门德尔松，在柏林猎人大厅于 1826 年 11 月 14 日用钢琴演奏。瓦格纳在莱比锡大学读书时，全部手抄过；且在 1830 年 10 月 6 日致书出版商肖特，提议由他把交响曲改成钢琴曲。可以说《第九交响曲》决定了瓦格纳的生涯。

③ 1824 年 9 月 17 日致肖特兄弟信中，贝多芬写道："艺术之神还不愿死亡把我带走；因为我还负欠甚多！在我出发去天国之前，必得把精灵启示我而要我完成的东西留给后人，我觉得我才开始写了几个音符。"《贝多芬书信集》二七二。

④ 1827 年 3 月 18 日贝多芬写信给莫舍勒斯说："初稿全部写成的一部交响曲和一支前奏曲放在我的书桌上。"但这部初稿从未发现。我们只在他的笔记上读到：

（转下页）

为格里尔巴策的《曼吕西纳》谱的音乐[1]，为克尔纳的《奥德赛》、歌德的《浮士德》谱的音乐[2]，《大卫与扫罗的清唱剧》，这些都表示他的精神倾向于德国古代大师的清明恬静之境：巴赫与亨德尔——尤其是倾向于南方，法国南部，或他梦想要去游历的意大利。[3]

施皮勒医生于1826年看见他，说他气色变得快乐而旺盛了。同年，当格里尔巴策最后一次和他晤面时，倒是贝多芬来鼓励这颓丧的诗人："啊，他说，要是我能有千分之一的你的体力和强毅的话！"时代是艰苦的。专制政治的反动，压迫着思想界。格里尔巴策呻吟道："言论检查

（接上页）"用 Andante（行板）写的 Cantique，——用古音阶写的宗教歌，或是用独立的形式，或是作为一支赋格曲的引子。这部交响曲的特点是引进歌唱，或者用在终局，或从 Adagio（柔板）起就插入。乐队中小提琴……等等，都当特别加强最后几段的力量。歌唱开始时一个一个地，或在最后几段中复唱 Adagio（柔板）——Adagio（柔板）的歌词用一个希腊神话或宗教颂歌，Allegro（快板）则用酒神庆祝的形式。"（以上见1818年笔记）由此可见以合唱终局的计划是预备用在第十而非第九交响曲的。

后来他又说要在《第十交响曲》中，把现代世界和古代世界调和起来，像歌德在第二部《浮士德》中所尝试的。

[1] 诗人原作是叙述一个骑士，恋爱着一个女神而被她拘囚着；他念着家乡与自由，这首诗和《汤豪舍》（译注：系瓦格纳的名歌剧）颇多相似之处，贝多芬在1823—1826年间曾经从事工作。

[2] 贝多芬从1808起就有意为《浮士德》写音乐。（《浮士德》以悲剧的形式出现是1807年秋。）这是他一生最重视的计划之一。

[3] 贝多芬的笔记中有："法国南部！对啦！对啦！""离开这里，只要办到这一着，你便能重新登上你艺术的高峰……写一部交响曲，然后出发，出发，出发……夏天，为了旅费工作着，然后周游意大利，西西里，和几个旁的艺术家一起……"（出处同前）

把我杀害了。倘使一个人要言论自由，思想自由，就得往北美洲去。"但没有一种权力能钳制贝多芬的思想。诗人库夫纳写信给他说："文字是被束缚了；幸而声音还是自由的。"贝多芬是伟大的自由之声，也许是当时德意志思想界唯一的自由之声。他自己也感到。他时常提起，他的责任是把他的艺术来奉献于"可怜的人类"，"将来的人类"，为他们造福利，给他们勇气，唤醒他们的迷梦，斥责他们的懦怯。他写信给侄子说："我们的时代，需要有力的心灵把这些可怜的人群加以鞭策。"1827年，米勒医生说"贝多芬对于政府、警察、贵族，永远自由发表意见，甚至在公众面前也是如此。[①]警察当局明明知道，但对他的批评和嘲讽认为无害的梦呓，因此也就让这个光芒四射的天才太平无事"。[②]

———————

[①] 在谈话手册里，我们可以读到（1819年份的）："欧洲政治目前所走的路，令人没有金钱没有银行便什么事都不能做。""统治者的贵族，什么也不曾学得，什么也不曾忘记。""五十年内，世界上到处都将有共和国。"

[②] 1819年他几被警察当局起诉，因为他公然声言："归根结底，基督不过是一个被钉死的犹太人。"那时他正写着《D调弥撒曲》。由此可见他的宗教感应是极其自由的。他在政治方面也是一样的毫无顾忌，很大胆地抨击他的政府之腐败。他特别指斥几件事情：法院组织的专制与依附权势，程序烦琐，完全妨害诉讼的进行；警权的滥用；官僚政治的腐化与无能；颓废的贵族享有特权，霸占着国家最高的职位。从1815年起，他在政治上是同情英国的。据申德勒说，他非常热烈地读着英国国会的记录。英国的乐队指挥西普里亚尼·波特于1817年来到维也纳，他说："贝多芬用尽一切诅咒的字眼痛骂奥国政府。他一心要到英国来看看下院的情况。他说：'你们英国人，你们的脑袋的确在肩膀上。'"

（转下页）

因此，什么都不能使这股不可驯服的力量屈膝。如今它似乎玩弄痛苦了。在此最后几年中所写的音乐，虽然环境恶劣，①往往有一副簇新的面目，嘲弄的，睥睨一切的，快乐的。他逝世以前四个月，在 1826 年 11 月完成的作品，作品第一三〇号的四重奏的新的结束是非常轻快的。实在这种快乐并非一般人所有的那种。时而是莫舍勒斯所说的嬉笑怒骂；时而是战胜了如许痛苦以后的动人的微笑。总之，他是战胜了。他不相信死。

然而死终于来了。1826 年 11 月终，他得着肋膜炎性的感冒；为侄子奔走前程而旅行回来，他在维也纳病倒了。②

（接上页）译注：1814 年拿破仑失败，列强举行维也纳会议，重行瓜分欧洲。奥国首相梅特涅雄心勃勃，颇有只手左右天下之志。对于奥国内部，厉行压迫，言论自由剥削殆尽。其时欧洲各国类皆趋于反动统治，虐害共和党人。但法国大革命的精神早已弥漫全欧，到处有蠢动之象。1820 年的西班牙、葡萄牙、那不勒斯的革命开其端，1821 年的希腊独立战争接踵而至，降至 1830 年法国又有七月革命，1848 年又有二月革命……贝多芬晚年的政治思想，正反映 1814—1830 年间欧洲知识分子的反抗精神。读者于此，必须参考当时国际情势，方能对贝多芬的思想有一估价准确之认识。

① 例如侄子之自杀。

② 他的病有两个阶段：（一）肺部的感冒，那是六天就结束的。"第七天上，他觉得好了一些，从床上起来，走路，看书，写作。"（二）消化器病，外加循环系病。医生说："第八天，我发现他脱了衣服，身体发黄色。剧烈地泄泻，外加呕吐，几乎使他那天晚上送命。"从那时起，水肿病开始加剧。这一次的复病还有我们迄今不甚清楚的精神上的原因。华洛赫医生说："一件使他愤慨的事，使他大发雷霆，非常苦恼，这就促成了病的爆发。打着寒噤，浑身抖战，因内脏的痛楚而起拘挛。"关于贝多芬最后一次的病情，从 1842 年起就有医生详细的叙述公开发表。

朋友都在远方。他打发侄儿去找医生。据说这麻木不仁的家伙竟忘记了使命，两天之后才重新想起来。医生来得太迟，而且治疗得很恶劣。三个月内，他运动家般的体格和病魔挣扎着。1827年1月3日，他把至爱的侄儿立为正式的承继人。他想到莱茵河畔的亲爱的友人；写信给韦格勒说："我多想和你谈谈！但我身体太弱了，除了在心里拥抱你和你的洛亨①以外，我什么都无能为力了。"要不是几个豪侠的英国朋友，贫穷的苦难几乎笼罩到他生命的最后一刻。他变得非常柔和，非常忍耐。②1827年2月17日，躺在弥留的床上，经过了三次手术以后，等待着第四次，③他在等待期间还安详地说："我耐着性子，想道：一切灾难都带来几分善。"

这个善，是解脱，是像他临终时所说的"喜剧的终场"——我们却说是他一生悲剧的终场。

他在大风雨中，大风雪中，一声响雷中，咽了最后一口气。一只陌生的手替他阖上了眼睛（1827年3月26日）。④

---

① 译注：洛亨即为韦格勒夫人埃莱奥诺雷的亲密的称呼。

② 一个名叫路德维希·克拉莫利尼的歌唱家，说他看见最后一次病中的贝多芬，觉得他心地宁静，慈祥恺恻，达于极点。

③ 据格哈得·冯·布罗伊宁的信，说他在弥留时，在床上受着臭虫的骚扰。——他的四次手术是1826年12月20日，1827年1月8日、2月2日和2月27日。

④ 这陌生人是青年音乐家安塞尔姆·许滕布伦纳。——布罗伊宁写道："感谢上帝！感谢他结束了这长时期悲惨的苦难。"

贝多芬的手稿、书籍、家具，全部拍卖掉，代价不过一五七五弗洛令。拍卖目录上登记着二五二件音乐手稿和音乐书籍，共售九八二弗洛令。谈话手册只售一弗洛令二十。

亲爱的贝多芬！多少人已颂赞过他艺术上的伟大。但他远不止是音乐家中的第一人，而是近代艺术的最英勇的力。对于一般受苦而奋斗的人，他是最大而最好的朋友。当我们对着世界的劫难感到忧伤时，他会到我们身旁来，好似坐在一个穿着丧服的母亲旁边，一言不发，在琴上唱着他隐忍的悲歌，安慰那哭泣的人。当我们对德与善的庸俗，斗争到疲惫的辰光，到此意志与信仰的海洋中浸润一下，将获得无可言喻的裨益。他分赠我们的是一股勇气，一种奋斗的欢乐，①一种感到与神同在的醉意。仿佛在他和大自然不息的沟通之下，②他竟感染了自然的深邃的力。格里尔巴策对贝多芬是钦佩之中含有惧意的，在提及他时说："他所到达的那种境界，艺术竟和犷野与古怪的原子混合为一。"舒曼提到《第五交响曲》时也说："尽管你时常听到它，它对你始终有一股不变的威力，有如自然界的现象，虽然时时发生，总教人充满着恐惧与惊异。"他的密友申德勒说："他抓住了大自然的精神。"——这是不错的：贝多芬是自然界的一股力；一种原始的力和大自然其余的部分接战之下，便产生了荷马史诗般的壮观。

---

① 他致"不朽的爱人"信中有言："当我有所克服的时候，我总是快乐的。"1801 年 11 月 16 日致韦格勒信中又言："噢！能把生命活上千百次真是多美——我非生来过恬静的日子的。"

② 申德勒有言："贝多芬教了我大自然的学问，在这方面的研究，他给我的指导和在音乐方面没有分别。使我陶醉的并非自然的律令 Law，而是自然的基本威力。"

他的一生宛如一天雷雨的日子。——先是一个明净如水的早晨。仅仅有几阵懒懒的微风。但在静止的空气中，已经有隐隐的威胁，沉重的预感。然后，突然之间巨大的阴影卷过，悲壮的雷吼，充满着声响的可怖的静默，一阵复一阵的狂风，《英雄交响曲》与《第五交响曲》。然而白日的清纯之气尚未受到损害。欢乐依然是欢乐，悲哀永远保存着一缕希望。但自1810年后，心灵的均衡丧失了。日光变得异样。最清楚的思想，也看来似乎水汽一般在升华：忽而四散，忽而凝聚，它们的又凄凉又古怪的骚动，罩住了心；往往乐思在薄雾之中浮沉了一二次以后，完全消失了，淹没了，直到曲终才在一阵狂飙中重新出现。即是快乐本身也蒙上苦涩与犷野的性质。所有的情操里都混合着一种热病，一种毒素。①黄昏将临，雷雨也随着酝酿。随后是沉重的云，饱蓄着闪电，给黑夜染成乌黑，挟带着大风雨，那是《第九交响曲》的开始。——突然，当风狂雨骤之际，黑暗裂了缝，夜在天空给赶走，由于意志之力，白日的清明重又还给了我们。

什么胜利可和这场胜利相比？波拿巴的哪一场战争，奥斯特利茨②哪一天的阳光，曾经达到这种超人的努力的光荣？曾经获得这种心灵从未获得的凯旋？一个不幸的人，贫穷，残废，孤独，由痛苦造成的人，世界不给他欢乐，他却创造了欢乐来给予世界！他用他的苦难来铸成欢

---

① 贝多芬1810年5月2日致韦格勒书中有言："噢，人生多美，但我的是永远受着毒害……"

② 译注：系拿破仑1805年12月大获胜利之地。

乐，好似他用那句豪语来说明的，——那是可以总结他一生，可以成为一切英勇心灵的箴言的：

用痛苦换来的欢乐。①

---

① 1815 年 10 月 19 日贝多芬致埃尔德迪夫人书。

贝多芬半身像

雨果·哈根创作，1892 年

贝多芬遗嘱

(A Lichnowsky, 21 septembre 1814)

"孤独，孤独，孤独"
1814 年 9 月 21 日致李希诺夫斯基

海林根施塔特遗嘱[①]
给我的兄弟卡尔与约翰·贝多芬

　　噢，你们这般人，把我当作或使人把我看作心怀怨恨的，疯狂的，或愤世嫉俗的，他们真是诬蔑了我！你们不知道在那些外表之下的隐秘的理由！从童年起，我的心和精神都倾向于慈悲的情操。甚至我老是准备去完成一些伟大的事业。可是你们想，六年以来我的身体何等恶劣，没有头脑的医生加深了我的病，年复一年地受着骗，空存着好转的希望，终于不得不看到一种"持久的病症"，即使痊愈不是完全无望，也得要长久的年代。生就一副热烈与活动的性格，甚至也能适应社会的消遣，我却老早被迫和人类分离，过着孤独生活。如果有时我要克服这一切，噢！总是被我残废这个悲惨的经验挡住了路！可是我不能对人说："讲得高声一些，叫喊吧；因为我是聋子！"啊！我怎能让人知道我的"一种感官"出了毛病，这感官在我是应该特别比人优胜，而我从前这副感官确比音乐界中谁都更完满的！——噢！这我办不到！——所以倘你们看见我孤僻自处，请你们原谅，因为我心中是要和人们做伴的。我

————————

① 海林根施塔特为维也纳近郊小镇名。贝多芬在此曾做勾留。

的灾祸对我是加倍的难受，因为我因之被人误解。在人群的交接中，在微妙的谈话中，在彼此的倾吐中去获得安慰，于我是禁止的。孤独，完全的孤独。越是我需要在社会上露面，越是我不能冒险。我只能过着亡命者的生活。如果我走近一个集团，我的心就惨痛欲裂，唯恐人家发觉我的病。因此我最近在乡下住了六个月。我的高明的医生劝我尽量保护我的听觉，他迎合我的心意。然而多少次我觉得非与社会接近不可时，我就禁不住要去了。但当我旁边的人听到远处的笛声而"我听不见"时，或"他听见牧童歌唱"而我一无所闻时，真是何等的屈辱！①这一类的经验几乎使我完全陷于绝望：我的不致自杀也是间不容发的事了。——"是艺术"，就只是艺术留住了我。啊！在我尚未把我感到的使命全部完成之前，我觉得不能离开这个世界。这样我总挨延着这种悲惨的——实在是悲惨的——生活，这个如是虚弱的身体，些少变化就曾使健康变为疾病的身体！——"忍耐啊！"——人家这么说着，我如今也只能把它来当作我的向导了。我已经有了耐性。——但愿我抵抗的决心长久支持，直到无情的死神来割断我的生

---

① 原关于这段痛苦的怨叹，我要提出一些意见，为谁都不曾提过的。大家知道在《田园交响曲》第二章之末，乐队奏出夜莺、杜鹃、鹌鹑的歌声；而且可说整个交响曲都是用自然界的歌唱与呓语组成的。美学家们发表过许多议论，要决定应否赞成这一类模仿音乐的尝试。没有一个人注意到贝多芬实在并未模仿，既然他什么都已无法听见：他只在精神上重造一个于他已经死灭的世界。就是这一点使他乐章中唤引起群鸟歌唱的部分显得如此动人。要听到它们的唯一的方法，是使它们在他心中歌唱。

命线的时候。——也许这倒更好，也许并不：总之我已端整好了。——二十八岁上，我已不得不看破一切，这不是容易的；保持这种态度，在一个艺术家比别人更难。

神明啊！你在天上参透着我的心，你认识它，你知道它对人类抱着热爱，抱着行善的志愿！噢，人啊，要是你们有一天读到这些，别忘记你们曾对我不公平；但愿不幸的人，看见一个与他同样的遭难者，不顾自然的阻碍，竭尽所能地厕身于艺术家与优秀之士之列，而能借以自慰。

你们，我的兄弟卡尔和约翰，我死后倘施密特教授尚在人世的话，用我的名义去请求他，把我的病状详细叙述，在我的病史之外再加上现在这封信，使社会在我死后尽可能地和我言归于好。——同时我承认你们是我的一些薄产的承继者。公公平平地分配，和睦相爱，缓急相助。你们给我的损害，你们知道我久已原谅。你，兄弟卡尔，我特别感谢你近来对我的忠诚。我祝望你们享有更幸福的生活，不像我这样充满着烦恼。把"德行"教给你们的孩子：使人幸福的是德行而非金钱。这是我的经验之谈。在患难中支持我的是道德，使我不曾自杀的，除了艺术以外也是道德。——别了，相亲相爱吧！——我感谢所有的朋友，特别是李希诺夫斯基亲王和施密特教授。——我希望李希诺夫斯基的乐器能保存在你们之中任何一个的手里。①但切勿因之而有何争论。倘能有助于你们，那么尽管卖掉它，不必迟疑。要是我在墓内还能帮助你们，我将何等欢喜！

---

① 译注：系指李氏送给他的一套弦乐四重奏乐器。

若果如此，我将怀着何等的欢心飞向死神。——倘使死神在我不及发展我所有的官能之前便降临，那么，虽然我命途多舛，我还嫌它来得过早，我祝祷能展缓它的出现。——但即使如此，我也快乐了。它岂非把我从无穷的痛苦之中解放了出来？——死亡愿意什么时候来就什么时候来吧，我将勇敢地迎接你。——别了，切勿把我在死亡中完全忘掉；我是值得你们思念的，因为我在世时常常思念你们，想使你们幸福。但愿你们幸福！

路德维希·凡·贝多芬
1802 年 10 月 6 日海林根施塔特

给我的兄弟卡尔和约翰在我死后开拆并执行

海林根施塔特，1802 年 10 月 10 日。——这样，我向你们告别了，——当然是很伤心地。——是的，我的希望，——至少在某程度内痊愈的希望，把我遗弃了。好似秋天的树叶摇落枯萎一般，——这希望于我也枯萎死灭了。几乎和我来时一样。——我去了。——即是最大的勇气，——屡次在美妙的夏天支持过我的，它也消逝了。——噢，万能的主宰，给我一天纯粹的快乐吧！——我没有听到欢乐的深远的声音已经多久！——噢！什么时候，噢，神明！什么时候我再能在自然与人类的庙堂中感觉到欢乐？——永远不？——不！——噢！这太残酷了！

书信集

贝多芬画像（44 岁）

路易·勒特恩（Louis Letronne）

依据布莱斯·霍费尔（Blasius Hoefel）版画绘制，1814 年

贝多芬致阿门达牧师书①

我的亲爱的，我的善良的阿门达，我的心坎里的朋友：

接读来信，我心中又是痛苦又是欢喜。你对于我的忠实和恳挚，能有什么东西可以相比？噢！你始终对我抱着这样的友情，真是太好了。是的，我把你的忠诚做过试验，而我是能把你和别个朋友辨别的。你不是一个维也纳的朋友，不，你是我的故乡所能产生的人物之一！我多祝望你能常在我身旁！因为你的贝多芬可怜已极。得知道我的最高贵的一部分，我的听觉，大大地衰退了。当你在我身边时，我已觉得许多征象，我瞒着；但从此越来越恶化。是否会医好，目前还不得而知；这大概和我肚子的不舒服有关。但那差不多已经痊愈；可是我的听觉还有告痊之望么？我当然如此希望；但非常渺茫，因为这一类的病是无药可治的。我得过着凄凉的生活，避免我一切心爱的人物，尤其是在这个如此可怜、如此自私的世界上！……——在所有的人中，我可以说最可靠的朋友是李希诺夫斯基。自从去年到现在，他给了我六百弗洛令；这个数目之外，再加上我作品售得的钱，使我不致为每天的面包发愁了。我如

———————————
① 时期约为 1801 年。

今所写的东西，立刻可有四五家出版商要，卖得很好的代价。——我近来写了不少东西；既然我知道你在××铺子里定购钢琴，我可把各种作品和钢琴一起打包寄给你，使你少费一些钱。

现在，我的安慰是来了一个朋友，和他我可享受一些谈心的乐趣，和纯粹的友谊：那是少年时代的朋友之一。[①]我和他时常谈到你，我告诉他，自从我离了家乡以后，你是我衷心选择的朋友之一。——他也不欢喜××；他素来太弱，担当不了友谊。[②]我把他和××完全认为高兴时使用一下的工具：但他们永远不能了解我崇高的活动，也不能真心参加我的生活；我只依着他们为我所尽的力而报答他们。噢！我将多幸福，要是我能完满地使用我的听觉的话！那时我将跑到你面前来。但我不得不远离着一切；我最美好的年龄虚度了，不曾实现我的才具与力量所能胜任的事情。——我不得不在伤心的隐忍中找栖身！固然我曾发愿要超临这些祸害；但又如何可能？是的，阿门达，倘六个月内我的病不能告痊，我要求你丢下一切而到我这里来；那时我将旅行（我的钢琴演奏和作曲还不很受到残废的影响；只有在与人交际时才特别不行）；你将做我的旅伴：我确信幸福不会缺少；现在有什么东西我不能与之一较短长？自你走后，我什么都写，连歌剧和宗教音乐都有。

是的，你是不会拒绝的，你会帮助你的朋友担受他的疾病和忧虑。我的钢琴演奏也大有进步，我也希望这旅行

① 斯特凡·冯·布罗伊宁。
② 疑系指兹梅什卡尔，他在维也纳当官廷秘书，对贝多芬极忠诚。

能使你愉快。然后，你永久留在我身旁。——你所有的信我全收到；虽然我复信极少，你始终在我眼前；我的心也以同样的温情为你跳动着。——关于我听觉的事，请严守秘密，对谁都勿提。——多多来信。即使几行也能使我安慰和得益。希望不久就有信来，我最亲爱的朋友。——我没有把你的四重奏①寄给你，因为从我知道正式写作四重奏之后，已把它大为修改：将来你自己会看到的。

　　——如今，别了，亲爱的好人！倘我能替你做些使你愉快的事，不用说你当告诉忠实的贝多芬，他是真诚地爱你的。

---

① 作品第十八号之一。

致弗兰茨·格哈得·韦格勒书

维也纳，1801 年 6 月 29 日

我的亲爱的好韦格勒：

多谢你的关注！我真是不该受，而且我的行为也不配受你的关注；然而你竟如此好心，即是我不可原恕的静默也不能使你沮丧；你永远是忠实的、慈悲的、正直的朋友。——说我能忘记你，忘记你们，忘记我如是疼爱如是珍视的你们，不，这是不可信的！有时我热烈地想念你们，想在你们旁边消磨若干时日。——我的故乡，我出生的美丽的地方，至今清清楚楚的在我眼前，和我离开你们时一样。当我能重见你们，向我们的父亲莱茵致敬时，将是我一生最幸福的岁月的一部分。——何时能实现，我还不能确言。——至少我可告诉你们，那时你将发觉我更长大：不说在艺术方面，而是在为人方面，你们将发觉我更善良更完满；如果我们的国家尚未有何进步，我的艺术应当用以改善可怜的人们的命运……

你要知道一些我的近况，那么，还不坏。从去年起，李希诺夫斯基（虽然我对你说了你还觉得难于相信）一直是我最热烈的朋友——（我们中间颇有些小小的误会，但更加强了我们的友谊）——他给我每年六百弗洛令的津贴，直到将来我找到一个相当的差事时为止。我的乐曲替我挣了不少钱，竟可说人家预定的作品使我有应接不暇之势。每件作品有六七个出版商争着要。人家不再跟我还价了；我定了一个价目，人家便照付。你瞧这多美妙。譬如我看

见一个朋友陷入窘境，倘我的钱袋不够帮助他；我只消坐在书桌前面；顷刻之间便解决了他的困难。——我也比从前更省俭了……

不幸，嫉妒的恶魔，我的羸弱的身体，竟来和我作难。三年以来，我的听觉逐渐衰退。这大概受我肚子不舒服的影响，那是你知道我以前已经有过，而现在更加恶劣的；因为我不断地泄泻，接着又是极度的衰弱。法朗克想用补药来滋补我，用薄荷油来医治我的耳朵。可是一无用处；听觉越来越坏，肚子也依然如故。这种情形一直到去年秋天，那时我常常陷于绝望。一个其蠢似驴的医生劝我洗冷水浴；另一个比较聪明的医生，劝我到多瑙河畔去洗温水浴：这倒大为见效。肚子好多了，但我的耳朵始终如此，或竟更恶化。去年冬天，我的身体简直糟透：我患着剧烈的腹痛，完全是复病的样子。这样一直到上个月，我去请教韦林；因为我想我的病是该请外科医生诊治的，而且我一直相信他。他差不多完全止住我的泄泻，又劝我洗温水浴，水里放一些健身的药酒；他不给我任何药物，直到四天前才给我一些治胃病药丸，和治耳朵的一种茶。我觉得好了一些，身体也强壮了些；只有耳朵轰轰作响，日夜不息。两年来我躲避一切交际，我不能对人说："我是聋子。"倘我干着别种职业，也许还可以；但在我的行当里，这是可怕的遭遇。敌人们将怎么说呢，而且他们的数目又是相当可观！①

使你对我这古怪的耳聋有个概念起计，我告诉你，在

---

① 这段文字"两年来……相当可观！"与前面第 12 页上对这封信的这段文字的引用，在字句表述上略有不同，各自保持原样不变！

戏院内我得坐在贴近乐队的地方才能懂得演员的说话。我听不见乐器和歌唱的高音，假如座位稍远的话。在谈话里，有些人从未觉察我的病，真是奇怪。人家柔和地谈话时，我勉强听到一些；是的，我听到声音，却听不出字句；但当人家高声叫喊时，我简直痛苦难忍了。结果如何，只有老天知道。韦林说一定会好转，即使不能完全复原。——我时常诅咒我的生命和我的造物主。普卢塔克教我学习隐忍，我却要和我的命运挑战，只要可能；但有些时候我竟是上帝最可怜的造物。——我求你勿把我的病告诉任何人，连对洛亨都不要说；我是把这件事情当作秘密般交托给你的。你能写信给韦林讨论这个问题，我很高兴。倘我的现状要持续下去，我将在明春到你身边来；你可在什么美丽的地方替我租一所乡下屋子，我愿重做六个月的乡下人。也许这对我有些好处。隐忍！多伤心的栖留所！然而这是我唯一的出路！——原谅我在你所有的烦恼中再来加上一重友谊的烦恼。

斯特凡·布罗伊宁此刻在这里，我们几乎天天在一起。回念当年的情绪，使我非常安慰！他已长成为一个善良而出色的青年，颇有些智识，（且像我们一样，）心地很纯正……

我也想写信给洛亨。即使我毫无音信，我也没有忘掉你们之中任何一个，亲爱的好人们；但是写信，你知道，素来非我所长；我最好的朋友都成年累月的接不到我一封信。我只在音符中过生活；一件作品才完工，另一件又已开始。照我现在的工作方式，我往往同时写着三四件东西。——时时来信吧；我将寻出一些时间来回答你。替我问候大家……

别了，我的忠实的，好韦格勒。相信你的贝多芬的情爱与友谊。

致韦格勒书

维也纳，1801 年 11 月 16 日

我的好韦格勒！

谢谢你对我表示的新的关切，尤其因为我的不该承受。——你要知道我身体怎样，需要什么。虽然谈论这个问题于我是那么不快，但我极乐意告诉你。

韦林几个月来老把发泡药涂在我的两臂上……这种治疗使我极端不快；痛苦是不必说，我还要一两天不能运用手臂……得承认耳朵里的轰轰声比从前轻减了些，尤其是左耳，那最先发病的一只；但我的听觉，迄今为止丝毫没有改善；我不敢决定它是否变得更坏。——肚子好多了；特别当我洗了几天温水浴后，可有八天或十天的舒服。每隔多少时候，我服用一些强胃的药；我也遵从你的劝告，把草药敷在腹上。——韦林不愿我提到淋雨浴。此外我也不大乐意他。他对于这样的一种病实在太不当心太不周到了，倘我不到他那边去，——而这于我又是多费事——就从来看不见他。——你想施密特如何？我不是乐于换医生；但似乎韦林太讲究手术，不肯从书本上去补充他的学识。——在这一点上施密特显得完全两样，也许也不像他那么大意。——人家说直流电有神效；你以为怎样？有一个医生告诉我，他看见一个聋而且哑的孩子恢复听觉，一个聋了七年的人也医好。——我正听说施密特在这方面有过经验。

我的生活重又愉快了些；和人们来往也较多了些。你

简直难于相信我两年来过的是何等孤独与悲哀的生活。我的残疾到处挡着我，好似一个幽灵，而我逃避着人群。旁人一定以为我是憎恶人类，其实我并不如此！——如今的变化，是一个亲爱的、可人的姑娘促成的；她爱我，我也爱她；这是两年来我重又遇到的幸福的日子；也是第一次我觉得婚姻可能给人幸福。不幸，她和我境况不同；——而现在，老实说我还不能结婚：还得勇敢地挣扎一下才行。要不是为了我的听觉，我早已走遍半个世界；而这是我应当做的。——琢磨我的艺术，在人前表现：对我再没更大的愉快了。——勿以为我在你们家里会快乐。谁还能使我快乐呢？连你们的殷勤，于我都将是一种重负：我将随时在你们脸上看到同情的表示，使我更苦恼。——我故园的美丽的乡土，什么东西在那里吸引我呢？不过是环境较好一些的希望罢了；而这个希望，倘没有这病，早已实现的了！噢！要是我能摆脱这病魔，我愿拥抱世界！我的青春，是的，我觉得它不过才开始；我不是一向病着么？近来我的体力和智力突飞猛进。我窥见我不能加以肯定的目标，我每天都更迫近它一些。唯有在这种思想里，你的贝多芬方能存活。一些休息都没有！——除了睡眠以外，我不知还有什么休息；而可怜我对睡眠不得不花费比从前更多的时间。但愿我能在疾病中解放出一半，那时候——我将以一个更能自主、更成熟的人的姿态，来到你们面前，加强我们永久的友谊。

我应当尽可能地在此世得到幸福——决不要苦恼。——不，这是我不能忍受的！我要扼住命运的咽喉。

它决不能使我完全屈服。——噢！能把生命活上千百次真是多美！——我非生来过恬静的日子的。

……替我向洛亨致千万的情意……——你的确有些爱我的，不是吗？相信我的情爱和友谊。

　　　　　　　　　　　　你的　贝多芬

韦格勒与埃莱奥诺雷·冯·布罗伊宁致贝多芬书[①]
科布伦茨，1825 年 12 月 28 日

亲爱的老友路德维希：

在我送里斯[②]的十个儿子之一上维也纳的时候，不由不想起你。从我离开维也纳二十八年以来，如果你不曾每隔两月接到一封长信，那么你该责备在我给你第一批信以后你的缄默。这是不可以的，尤其是现在；因为我们这般老年人多乐意在过去中讨生活，我们最大的愉快莫过于青年时代的回忆。至少对于我，由于你的母亲（上帝祝福她！）之力而获致的对你的认识和亲密的友谊，是我一生光明的一点，为我乐于回顾的……我远远地瞩视你时，仿佛瞩视一个英雄似的，我可以自豪地说："我对他的发展并非全无影响；他曾对我吐露他的愿意和幻梦；后来当他常常被人误解时，我才明白他的志趣所在。"感谢上帝使我能和我的妻子谈起你，现在再和我的孩子们谈起你！对于你，我岳母的家比你自己的家还要亲切，尤其从你高贵的母亲死后。再和我们说一遍呀："是的，在欢乐中，在悲哀中，我都想念你们。"一个人即使像你这样升得高，一生也只有一次幸福：就是年轻的时光。波恩，克罗伊茨贝格，

---

① 作者认为在此插入以下两封书信并非没有意义，因为它们表现出这些卓越的人物，贝多芬最忠实的朋友。而且从朋友身上更可以认识贝多芬的面目。

② 译注：里斯（Ferdinand Ries, 1784—1838），德国钢琴家兼作曲家，贝多芬的学生和助手。

戈德斯贝格，佩比尼哀等等，应该是你的思念欢欣地眷恋的地方。

现在我要对你讲起我和我们，好让你写复信时有一个例子。

1796年从维也纳回来之后，我的境况不大顺利；好几年中我只靠了行医糊口；而在此可怜的地方，直要经过多少年月我才差堪温饱。以后我当了教授，有了薪给，1802年结了婚。一年以后我生了一个女儿，至今健在，教育也受完全了。她除了判断正直以外，秉受着她父亲清明的气质，她把贝多芬的奏鸣曲弹奏得非常动人。在这方面她不值得什么称誉，那完全是靠天赋。1807年，我有了一个儿子，现在柏林学医。四年之内，我将送他到维也纳来：你肯照顾他么？……今年八月里我过了六十岁的生辰，来了六十位左右的朋友和相识，其中有城里第一流的人物。从1807年起，我住在这里，如今我有一座美丽的屋子和一个很好的职位。上司对我表示满意，国王颁赐勋章和封绶。洛亨和我，身体都还不差。——好了，我已把我们的情形完全告诉了你，轮到你了！……

你永远不愿把你的目光从圣艾蒂安教堂①上移向别处吗？旅行不使你觉得愉快吗？你不愿再见莱茵了吗？——洛亨和我，向你表示无限恳切之意。

你的老友　韦格勒

① 译注：系维也纳名教堂之一。

科布伦茨，1825 年 12 月 29 日

亲爱的贝多芬，多少年来亲爱的人！

　　要韦格勒重新写信给您是我的愿望。——如今这愿望实现以后，我认为应当添加几句，——不但为特别使您回忆我，而且为加重我们的请求，问你是否毫无意思再见莱茵和您的出生地，——并且给韦格勒和我最大的快乐。我们的朗亨①感谢您给了她多少幸福的时间；——她多高兴听我们谈起您；——她详细知道我们青春时代在波恩的小故事，——争吵与和好……她将多少乐意看见您！——不幸这妮子毫无音乐天才；但她曾用过不少工夫，那么勤奋那么有恒，居然能弹奏您的奏鸣曲和变奏曲等等了；又因音乐对于韦始终是最大的安慰，所以她给他消磨了不少愉快的光阴。尤利乌斯颇有音乐才具，但目前还不知用功，——六个月以来，他很快乐地学习着大提琴；既然柏林有的是好教授，我相信他能有进步。——两个孩子都很高大，像父亲；——韦至今保持着的——感谢上帝！——和顺与快活的心情，孩子们也有。韦最爱弹您的变奏曲里的主题；老人们自有他们的嗜好，但他也奏新曲，而且往往用着难以置信的耐性。——您的歌，尤其为他爱好；韦从没有进他的房间而不坐上钢琴的。——因此，亲爱的贝多芬，您可看到，我们对您的思念是多么鲜明多么持久。——但望您告诉我们，说这对您多少有些价值，说我

---

① 译注：系她的女儿。

们不曾被您完全忘怀。——要不是我们最热望的意愿往往难于实现的话，我们早已到维也纳我的哥哥家里来探望您了；——但这旅行是不能希望的了，因为我们的儿子现在柏林。——韦已把我们的情况告诉了您：——我们是不该抱怨的了。——对于我们，连最艰难的时代也比对多数其余的人好得多。——最大的幸福是我们身体健康，有着很好而纯良的儿女。——是的，他们还不曾使我们有何难堪，他们是快乐的、善良的孩子。——朗亨只有一桩大的悲伤，即当我们可怜的布尔沙伊德死去的时候，——那是我们大家不会忘记的。别了，亲爱的贝多芬，请您用慈悲的心情想念我们吧。

埃莱奥诺雷·韦格勒

致韦格勒书①

维也纳，1826 年 10 月 7 日

亲爱的老朋友：

你和你洛亨的信给了我多少欢乐，我简直无法形容。当然我应该立刻回复的；但我生性疏懒，尤其在写信方面，因为我想最好的朋友不必我写信也能认识我。我在脑海里常常答复你们；但当我要写下来时，往往我把笔丢得老远，因为我不能写出我的感觉。我记得你一向对我表示的情爱，譬如你教人粉刷我的房间，使我意外地欢喜了一场。我也不忘布罗伊宁一家。彼此分离是事理之常：各有各的前程要趱奔；就只永远不能动摇的为善的原则，把我们永远牢固地连在一起。不幸今天我不能称心如意地给你写信，因为我躺在床上……

你的洛亨的倩影，一直在我的心头，我这样说是要你知道，我年青时代一切美好和心爱的成分于我永远是宝贵的。

……我的箴言始终是：无日不动笔；如果我有时让艺术之神瞌睡，也只为要使它醒后更兴奋。我还希望再留几件大作品在世界上；然后和老小孩一般，我将在一些好人

---

① 贝多芬答复韦格勒夫妇的信，已在十个月之后；可见当时的朋友，即使那样的相爱，他们的情爱也不像我们今日这样的急切。

中间结束我尘世的途程。[1]

……在我获得的荣誉里面——因为知道你听了会高兴，所以告诉你——有已故的法王赠我的勋章，镌着："王赠予贝多芬先生"；此外还附有一封非常客气的信，署名的是："王家侍从长，夏特勒大公"。

亲爱的朋友，今天就以这几行为满足吧。过去的回忆充满我的心头，寄此信的时候，我禁不住涕泪交流。这不过是一个引子；不久你可接到另一封信；而你来信越多，就越使我快活。这是无须疑惑的，当我们的交谊已到了这个田地的时候。别了。请你温柔地为我拥抱你亲爱的洛亨和孩子们。想念我啊。但愿上帝与你们同在！

永远尊敬你的，忠实的，真正的朋友。

贝多芬

---

[1] 贝多芬毫未想到那时他所写的，作品第一三〇号的四重奏的改作的终局部分，已是他最后的作品。那时他在兄弟家里，在多瑙河畔小镇上。

致韦格勒书

维也纳，1827 年 2 月 17 日

我的正直的老友：

我很高兴地从布罗伊宁那里接到你的第二封信。我身体太弱，不能作复；但你可想到，你对我所说的一切都是我欢迎而渴望的。至于我的复原，如果我可这样说的话，还很迟缓；虽然医生们没有说，我猜到还须施行第四次手术。我耐着性子，想道：一切灾难都带来几分善……今天我还有多少话想对你说！但我太弱了：除了在心里拥抱你和你的洛亨以外，什么都无能为力。你的忠实的老朋友对你和你一家表示真正的友谊和眷恋。

贝多芬

致莫舍勒斯书①

维也纳，1827年3月14日

我的亲爱的莫舍勒斯：

……2月17日，我受了第四次手术；现又发现确切的征象，需要不久等待第五次手术。长此以往，这一切如何结束呢？我将临到些什么？——我的一份命运真是艰苦已极。但我听任命运安排，只求上帝，以它神明的意志让我在生前受着死的磨难的期间，不再受生活的窘迫。这可使我有勇气顺从着至高的神的意志去担受我的命运，不论它如何艰苦，如何可怕。

……您的朋友

L.V. 贝多芬

---

① 贝多芬此时快要不名一文了，他写信给伦敦的音乐协会和当时在英国的莫舍勒斯，要求他们替他举办一个音乐会筹一笔款子。伦敦的音乐协会慷慨地立即寄给他一百镑作为预支。贝多芬衷心感动。据一个朋友说："他收到这封信的时候，合着双手，因快乐与感激而号啕大哭起来，在场的人都为之心碎。"感动之下，旧创又迸发了，但他还要念出信稿，教人写信去感谢"豪侠的英国人分担他悲惨的命运"；他答应他们制作一支大曲：《第十交响曲》，一支前奏曲，还有听他们指定就是。他说："我将心中怀着从未有过的热爱替他们写作那些乐曲。"这封复信是3月18日写的。同月26日他就死了。

贝多芬画像

恩里科·卡鲁索，1910 年

思想录

《月光曲》签名页（于贝多芬故居波恩）

关于音乐

没有一条规律不可为获致"更美"的效果起计而破坏。

音乐当使人类的精神爆出火花。

音乐是比一切智慧一切哲学更高的启示……谁能参透我音乐的意义，便能超脱寻常人无以振拔的苦难。

（1810年致贝蒂娜）

最美的事，莫过于接近神明而把它的光芒散播于人间。

为何我写作？——我心中所蕴蓄的必得流露出来，所以我才写作。

你相信吗：当神明和我说话时，我是想着一架神圣的提琴，而写下它所告诉我的一切？

（致舒潘齐希）

照我作曲的习惯，即在制作器乐的时候，我眼前也摆好着全部的轮廓。

（致特赖奇克）

不用钢琴而作曲是必须的……慢慢地可以养成一种机能，把我们所愿望的、所感觉的，清清楚楚映现出来，这对于高贵的灵魂是必不可少的。

（致奥太子鲁道夫）

描写是属于绘画的。在这一方面，诗歌和音乐比较之下，也可说是幸运的了；它的领域不像我的那样受限制；但另一方面，我的领土在旁的境界内扩张得更远；人家不能轻易达到我的王国。

（致威廉·格哈得）

自由与进步是艺术的目标，如在整个人生中一样。即使我们现代人不及我们祖先坚定，至少有许多事情已因文明的精炼而大为扩张。

（致奥太子鲁道夫）

我的作品一经完成，就没有再加修改的习惯。因为我深信部分的变换足以改易作品的性格。

（致汤姆森）

除了"荣耀归主"和类乎此的部分以外，纯粹的宗教音乐只能用声乐来表现。所以我最爱帕莱斯特里纳；但没有他的精神和他的宗教观念而去模仿他，是荒谬的。

（致大风琴手弗罗伊登贝格）

当你的学生在琴上指法适当，节拍准确，弹奏音符也相当合拍时，你只须留心风格，勿在小错失上去阻断他，而只等一曲终了时告诉他。——这个方法可以养成"音乐家"，而这是音乐艺术的第一个目的。[①]……至于表现技巧的篇章，可使他轮流运用全部手指……当然，手指用得较少时可以获得人家所谓"圆转如珠"的效果；但有时我们更爱别的宝物。

（致钢琴家车尔尼）

在古代大师里，唯有德国人亨德尔和赛巴斯蒂安·巴赫真有天才。

（1819 年致奥太子鲁道夫）

我整个的心为着赛巴斯蒂安·巴赫的伟大而崇高的艺术跳动，他是和声之王。

（1801 年致霍夫迈斯特）

---

① 1809 年特雷蒙男爵曾言："贝多芬的钢琴技术并不准确，指法往往错误；音的性质也被忽视。但谁会想到他是一个演奏家呢？人家完全沉浸在他的思想里，至于表现思想的他的手法，没有人加以注意。"

我素来是最崇拜莫扎特的人，直到我生命的最后一刻，我还是崇拜他的。

（1826 年致神父斯塔德勒）

　　我敬重您的作品，甚于一切旁的戏剧作品。每次我听到您的一件新作时，我总是非常高兴，比对我自己的更感兴趣：总之，我敬重您，爱您……您将永远是我在当代的人中最敬重的一个。如果您肯给我几行，您将给我极大的快乐和安慰。艺术结合人类，尤其是真正的艺术家们；也许您肯把我归入这个行列之内。①

（1823 年致凯鲁比尼）

---

① 这封信，我们以前提过，凯鲁比尼置之不理。

关于批评

在艺术家的立场上，我从没对别人涉及我的文字加以注意。

（1825 年致肖特）

我和伏尔泰一样地想："几个苍蝇咬几口，决不能羁留一匹英勇的奔马。"

（1826 年致克莱因）

至于那些蠢货，只有让他们去说。他们的嚼舌决不能使任何人不朽，也决不能使阿波罗指定的人丧失其不朽。

（1801 年致霍夫迈斯特）

附　录

贝多芬画像（48 岁）
克洛伯（Kloeber）创作

贝多芬的作品及其精神

傅 雷

一、贝多芬与力

十八世纪是一个兵连祸结的时代，也是歌舞升平的时代，是古典主义没落的时代，也是新生运动萌芽的时代——新陈代谢的作用在历史上从未停止：最混乱最秽浊的地方就有鲜艳的花朵在探出头来。法兰西大革命，展开了人类史上最惊心动魄的一页：十九世纪！多悲壮，多灿烂！仿佛所有的天才都降生在一时期……从拿破仑到俾斯麦，从康德到尼采，从歌德到左拉，从达维德到塞尚，从贝多芬到俄国五大家；北欧多了一个德意志；南欧多了一个意大利，民主和专制的搏斗方终，社会主义的殉难生活已经开始：人类几曾在一百年中走过这么长的路！而在此波澜壮阔、峰峦重叠的旅程的起点，照耀着一颗巨星：贝多芬。在音响的世界中，他预言了一个民族的复兴——德意志联邦，——他象征着一世纪中人类活动的基调——力！

一个古老的社会崩溃了，一个新的社会在酝酿中。在青黄不接的过程内，第一先得解放个人。①反抗一切约束，争取一切自由的个人主义，是未来世界的先驱。各有各的时代。第一是：我！然后是：社会。

要肯定这个"我"，在帝王与贵族之前解放个人，使他们承认个个人都是帝王贵族，或个个帝王贵族都是平民，就须先肯定"力"，把它栽培，扶养，提出，具体表现，使人不得不接受。每个自由的"我"要指挥。倘他不能在行动上，至少能在艺术上指挥。倘他不能征服王国像拿破仑，至少他要征服心灵、感觉和情操，像贝多芬。是的，贝多芬与力，这是一个天生就的题目。我们不在这个题目上作一番探讨，就难能了解他的作品及其久远的影响。

从罗曼·罗兰所作的传记里，我们已熟知他运动家般的体格。平时的生活除了过度艰苦以外，没有旁的过度足以摧毁他的健康。健康是他最珍视的财富，因为它是一切"力"的资源。当时见过他的人说"他是力的化身"，当然这是含有肉体与精神双重的意义的。他的几件无关紧要的性的冒险，②既未减损他对于爱情的崇高的理想，也未减损他对于肉欲的控制力。他说："要是我牺牲了我的生命力，还有什么可以留给高贵与优越？"力，是的，体格的力，道德的力，是贝多芬的口头禅。"力是那般与寻常人不同

---

① 这是文艺复兴发轫而未完成的基业。

② 这一点，我们无须为他隐讳。传记里说他终身童贞的话是靠不住的，罗曼·罗兰自己就修正过。贝多芬1816年的日记内就有过性关系的记载。

的人的道德，也便是我的道德。"①这种论调分明已是"超人"的口吻。而且在他三十岁前后，过于充溢的力未免有不公平的滥用。不必说他暴烈的性格对身份高贵的人要不时爆发，即对他平辈或下级的人也有枉用的时候。他胸中满是轻蔑：轻蔑弱者，轻蔑愚昧的人，轻蔑大众，②甚至轻蔑他所爱好而崇拜他的人。③在他青年时代帮他不少忙的李希诺斯夫基公主的母亲，曾有一次因为求他弹琴而下跪，他非但拒绝，甚至在沙发上立也不立起来。后来他和李希诺斯夫基亲王反目，临走时留下的条子是这样写的："亲王，您之为您，是靠了偶然的出身；我之为我，是靠了我自己。亲王们现在有的是，将来也有的是。至于贝多芬，却只有一个。"这种骄傲的反抗，不独用来对另一阶级和同一阶级的人，且也用来对音乐上的规律：

"照规则是不许把这些和弦连用在一块的……"人家和他说。

"可是我允许。"他回答。

然而读者切勿误会，切勿把常人的狂妄和天才的自信混为一谈，也切勿把力的过剩的表现和无理的傲慢视同一律。以上所述，不过是贝多芬内心蕴蓄的精力，因过于丰满之故而在行动上流露出来的一方面；而这一方面，——让我们说老实话——也并非最好的一方面。缺陷与过失，

① 1800年语。

② 然而他又是热爱人类的人！

③ 在他致阿门达牧师信内，有两句说话便是诬蔑一个对他永远忠诚的朋友的。参看《贝多芬书信集》。

在伟人身上也仍然是缺陷与过失。而且贝多芬对世俗对旁人尽管傲岸不逊，对自己却竭尽谦卑。当他对车尔尼谈着自己的缺点和教育的不够时，叹道："可是我并非没有音乐的才具！"二十岁时摒弃的大师，他四十岁上把一个一个的作品重新披读。晚年他更说："我才开始学得一些东西……"青年时，朋友们向他提起他的声名，他回答说："无聊！我从未想到声名和荣誉而写作。我心坎里的东西要出来，所以我才写作！"①

可是他精神的力，还得我们进一步去探索。

大家说贝多芬是最后一个古典主义者，又是最先一个浪漫主义者。浪漫主义者，不错，在表现为先，形式其次上面，在不避剧烈的情绪流露上面，在极度的个人主义上面，他是的。但浪漫主义的感伤气氛与他完全无缘，他生平最厌恶女性的男子。②和他性格最不相容的是没有逻辑和过分夸张的幻想。他是音乐家中最男性的。罗曼·罗兰甚至不大受得了女子弹奏贝多芬的作品，除了极少的例外。他的钢琴即兴，素来被认为具有神奇的魔力。当时极优秀的钢琴家里斯和车尔尼辈都说："除了思想的特异与优美之外，表情中间另有一种异乎寻常的成分。"他赛似狂风暴雨中的魔术师，会从"深渊里"把精灵呼召到"高峰上"。听众号啕大哭，他的朋友雷夏尔特流了不少热泪，没有一双眼睛不湿……当他弹完以后看见这些泪人儿时，他耸耸

① 这是车尔尼的记载。——这一段希望读者，尤其是音乐青年，作为座右铭。
② 编注：原文如此。

肩，放声大笑道："啊，疯子！你们真不是艺术家。艺术家是火，他是不哭的。"①又有一次，他送一个朋友远行时，说："别动感情。在一切事情上，坚毅和勇敢才是男儿本色。"这种控制感情的力，是大家很少认识的！"人家想把他这株橡树当作萧飒的白杨，不知萧飒的白杨是听众。他是力能控制感情的。"②

音乐家，光是做一个音乐家，就需要有对一个意念集中注意的力，需要西方人特有的那种控制与行动的铁腕：因为音乐是动的构造，所有的部分都得同时抓握。他的心灵必须在静止（immobilité）中作疾如闪电的动作。清明的目光，紧张的意志，全部的精神都该超临在整个梦境之上。那么，在这一点上，把思想抓握得如是紧密，如是恒久，如是超人式的，恐怕没有一个音乐家可和贝多芬相比。因为没有一个音乐家有他那样坚强的力。他一朝握住一个意念时，不到把它占有决不放手。他自称那是"对魔鬼的追逐"。——这种控制思想，左右精神的力，我们还可从一个较为浮表的方面获得引证。早年和他在维也纳同住过的赛弗里德曾说："当他听人家一支乐曲时，要在他脸上去猜测赞成或反对是不可能的；他永远是冷冷的，一无动静。精神活动是内在的，而且是无时或息的；但躯壳只像一块没有灵魂的大理石。"

要是在此灵魂的探险上更往前去，我们还可发现更深邃更神化的面目。如罗曼·罗兰所说的：提起贝多芬，不

---

① 以上均见车尔尼记载。

② 罗曼·罗兰语。

能不提起上帝。①贝多芬的力不但要控制肉欲，控制感情，控制思想，控制作品，且竟与运命挑战，与上帝搏斗。"他可把神明视为平等，视为他生命中的伴侣，被他虐待的；视为磨难他的暴君，被他诅咒的；再不然把它认为他的自我之一部，或是一个冷酷的朋友，一个严厉的父亲……而且不论什么，只要敢和贝多芬对面，他就永不和它分离。一切都会消逝，他却永远在它面前。贝多芬向它哀诉，向它怨艾，向它威逼，向它追问。内心的独白永远是两个声音的。从他初期的作品起，②我们就听见这些两重灵魂的对白，时而协和，时而争执，时而扭殴，时而拥抱……但其中之一总是主子的声音，决不会令你误会。"③倘没有这等持久不屈的"追逐魔鬼"、捯住上帝的毅力，他哪还能在"海林根施塔特遗嘱"之后再写《英雄交响曲》和《命运交响曲》？哪还能战胜一切疾病中最致命的——耳聋？

耳聋，对平常人是一部分世界的死灭，对音乐家是整个世界的死灭。整个的世界死灭了而贝多芬不曾死！并且他还重造那已经死灭的世界，重造音响的王国，不但为他自己，而且为着人类，为着"可怜的人类"！这样一种超生和创造的力，只有自然界里那种无名的、原始的力可以相比。在死亡包裹着一切的大沙漠中间，唯有自然的力才能给你一片水草！

①　注意：此处所谓上帝系指十八世纪泛神论中的上帝。

②　作品第九号之三的三重奏的 Allegro，作品第十八号之四的四重奏的第一章，及《悲怆奏鸣曲》等。

③　以上引罗曼·罗兰语。

1800年，十九世纪第一页。那时的艺术界，正如行动界一样，是属于强者而非属于微妙的机智的。谁敢保存他本来面目，谁敢威严地主张和命令，社会就跟着他走。个人的强项，直有吞噬一切之势；并且有甚于此的是：个人还需要把自己溶化在大众里，溶化在宇宙里。所以罗曼·罗兰把贝多芬和上帝的关系写得如是壮烈，绝不是故弄玄妙的文章，而是窥透了个人主义的深邃的意识。艺术家站在"无意识界"的最高峰上，他说出自己的胸怀，结果是唱出了大众的情绪。贝多芬不曾下功夫去认识的时代意识，时代意识就在他自己的思想里。拿破仑把自由、平等、博爱当作幌子踏遍了欧洲，实在还是替整个时代的"无意识界"做了代言人。感觉早已普遍散布在人们心坎间，虽有传统、盲目的偶像崇拜，竭力高压也是徒然，艺术家迟早会来揭幕！《英雄交响曲》！即在1800年以前，少年贝多芬的作品，对于当时的青年音乐界，也已不下于《少年维特之烦恼》那样的诱人。[①]然而《第三交响曲》是第一声洪亮的信号。力解放了个人，个人解放了大众，——自然，这途程还长得很，有待于我们，或以后几代的努力；但力的化身已经出现过，悲壮的例子写定在历史上，目前的问题不是否定或争辩，而是如何继续与完成……

　　当然，我不否认力是巨大无比的，巨大到可怕的东西。普罗米修斯的神话存在了已有二十余世纪。使大地上五谷丰登、果实累累的，是力；移山倒海，甚至使星球击撞的，

---

① 　莫舍勒斯说他少年在音乐院里私下问同学借抄贝多芬的《悲怆奏鸣曲》，因为教师是绝对禁止"这种狂妄的作品"的。

也是力！在人间如在自然界一样，力足以推动生命，也能促进死亡。两个极端摆在前面：一端是和平、幸福、进步、文明、美；一端是残杀、战争、混乱、野蛮、丑恶。具有"力"的人宛如执握着一个转折乾坤的钟摆，在这两极之间摆动。往哪儿去？……瞧瞧先贤的足迹吧。贝多芬的力所推动的是什么？锻炼这股力的洪炉又是什么？——受苦，奋斗，为善。没有一个艺术家对道德的修积，像他那样的兢兢业业；也没有一个音乐家的生涯，像贝多芬这样的酷似一个圣徒的行述。天赋给他的犷野的力，他早替它定下了方向。它是应当奉献于同情、怜悯、自由的；它是应当教人隐忍、舍弃、欢乐的。对苦难，命运，应当用"力"去反抗和征服；对人类，应当用"力"去鼓励，去热烈地爱。——所以《弥撒曲》里的泛神气息，代卑微的人类呼吁，为受难者歌唱……《第九交响曲》里的欢乐颂歌，又从痛苦与斗争中解放了人，扩大了人。解放与扩大的结果，人与神明迫近，与神明合一。那时候，力就是神，力就是力，无所谓善恶，无所谓冲突，力的两极性消灭了。人已超临了世界，跳出了万劫，生命已经告终，同时已经不朽！这才是欢乐，才是贝多芬式的欢乐！

二、贝多芬的音乐建树

现在，我们不妨从高远的世界中下来，看看这位大师在音乐艺术内的实际成就。

在这件工作内，最先仍须从回顾以往开始。一切的进步只能从比较上看出。十八世纪是讲究说话的时代，在无论何种艺术里，这是一致的色彩。上一代的古典精神至此变成纤巧与雕琢的形式主义，内容由微妙而流于空虚，由富丽而陷于贫弱。不论你表现什么，第一要"说得好"，要巧妙，雅致。艺术品的要件是明白、对称、和谐、中庸；最忌狂热、真诚、固执，那是"趣味恶劣"的表现。海顿的宗教音乐也不容许有何种神秘的气氛，它是空洞的，世俗气极浓的作品。因为时尚所需求的弥撒曲，实际只是一个变相的音乐会；由歌剧曲调与悦耳的技巧表现混合起来的东西，才能引起听众的趣味。流行的观念把人生看作肥皂泡，只顾享受和鉴赏它的五光十色，而不愿参透生与死的神秘。所以海顿的旋律是天真地、结实地构成的，所有的乐句都很美妙和谐；它特别魅惑你的耳朵，满足你的智的要求，却从无深切动人的言语诉说。即使海顿是一个善良的、虔诚的"好爸爸"，也逃不出时代感觉的束缚：缺乏热情。幸而音乐在当时还是后起的艺术，连当时那么浓厚的颓废色彩都阻遏不了它的生机。十八世纪最精彩的面目和最可爱的情调，还找到一个旷世的天才做代言人：莫扎特。他除了歌剧以外，在交响乐方面的贡献也不下于海顿，且在精神方面还更走前了一步。音乐之作为心理描写是从他开始的。他的《G小调交响曲》在当时批评界的心目中已是艰涩难解（!）之作。但他的温柔与妩媚，细腻入微的感觉，匀称有度的体裁，我们仍觉是旧时代的产物。

而这是不足为奇的。时代精神既还有最后几朵鲜花需要开放，音乐曲体大半也还在摸索着路子。所谓古奏鸣曲的形式，确定了不过半个世纪。最初，奏鸣曲的第一章只有一个主题（thème），后来才改用两个基调（tonalité）不同而互有关连的两个主题。当古典奏鸣曲的形式确定以后，就成为三鼎足式的对称乐曲，主要以三章构成，即：快——慢——快。第一章 Allegro 本身又含有三个步骤：（一）破题（exposition），即披露两个不同的主题；（二）发展（développement），把两个主题作种种复音的配合，作种种的分析或综合——这一节是全曲的重心；（三）复题（récapitulation），重行披露两个主题，而第二主题[1]以和第一主题相同的基调出现，因为结论总以第一主题的基调为本。[2]第二章 Andante 或 Adagio，或 Larghetto，以歌（Lied）体或变奏曲（Variation）写成。第三章 Allegro 或 Presto，和第一章同样用两句三段组成；再不然是 Rondo，由许多复奏（répétition）组成，而用对比的次要乐句作穿插。这就是三鼎足式的对称。但第二与第三章间，时或插入 Menuet 舞曲。

这个格式可说完全适应着时代的趣味。当时的艺术家首先要使听众对一个乐曲的每一部分都感兴味，而不为单

---

① 亦称副句，第一主题亦称主句。

② 这第一章部分称为奏鸣曲典型：forme-sonate。

独的任何部分着迷。①第一章 Allegro 的美的价值，特别在于明白、均衡和有规律：不同的乐旨总是对比的，每个乐旨总在规定的地方出现，它们的发展全在典雅的形式中进行。第二章 Andante，则来抚慰一下听众微妙精炼的感觉，使全曲有些优美柔和的点缀；然而一切剧烈的表情是给庄严稳重的 Menuet 挡住去路的，——最后再来一个天真的 Rondo，用机械式的复奏和轻盈的爱娇，使听的人不致把艺术当真，而明白那不过是一场游戏。渊博而不迂腐，敏感而不着魔，在各种情绪的表皮上轻轻拂触，却从不停留在某一固定的感情上：这美妙的艺术组成时，所模仿的是沙龙里那些翩翩蛱蝶，组成以后所供奉的也仍是这般翩翩蛱蝶。

我所以冗长地叙述这段奏鸣曲史，因为奏鸣曲②是一切交响曲、四重奏等纯粹音乐的核心。贝多芬在音乐上的创新也是由此开始。而且我们了解了他的奏鸣曲组织，对他一切旁的曲体也就有了纲领。古典奏鸣曲虽有明白与构造结实之长，但有呆滞单调之弊。乐旨（motif）与破题之间，乐节（période）与复题之间，凡是专司联络之职的过板（conduit）总是无美感与表情可言的。当乐曲之始，两个主题一经披露之后，未来的结论可以推想而知：起承转合的方式，宛如学院派的辩论一般有固定的线索，一言以蔽之，这是西洋音乐上的八股。

贝多芬对奏鸣曲的第一件改革，便是推翻它刻板的规

---

① 所以特别重视均衡。

② 尤其是其中奏鸣曲典型那部分。

条，给以范围广大的自由与伸缩，使它施展雄辩的机能。他的三十二阕钢琴奏鸣曲中，十三阕有四章，十三阕只有三章，六阕只有两章，每阕各章的次序也不依"快——慢——快"的成法。两个主题在基调方面的关系，同一章内各个不同的乐旨间的关系，都变得自由了。即是奏鸣曲的骨干——奏鸣曲典型——也被修改。连接各个乐旨或各个小段落的过板，到贝多芬手里大为扩充，且有了生气，有了更大的和更独立的音乐价值，甚至有时把第二主题的出现大为延缓，而使它以不重要的插曲的形式出现。前人作品中纯粹分立而仅有乐理关系①的两个主题，贝多芬使它们在风格上统一，或者出之以对照，或者出之以类似。所以我们在他作品中常常一开始便听到两个原则的争执，结果是其中之一获得了胜利；有时我们却听到两个类似的乐旨互相融和。②例如作品第七十一号之一的《告别奏鸣曲》，第一章内所有旋律的元素，都是从最初三音符上衍变出来的。奏鸣曲典型部分原由三个步骤组成，③贝多芬又于最后加上一节结局（coda），把全章乐旨作一有力的总结。

贝多芬在即兴（improvisation）方面的胜长，一直影响到他奏鸣曲的曲体。据约翰·桑太伏阿纳④的分析，贝多芬

---

① 即副句与主句互有关系，例如以主句基调的第五度音作为副句的主调音等等。

② 这就是上文所谓的两重灵魂的对白。

③ 详见前文。

④ 近代法国音乐史家。

在主句披露完后，常有无数的延音（point d'orgue），无数的休止，仿佛他在即兴时继续寻思，犹疑不决的神气。甚至他在一个主题的发展中间，会插入一大段自由的诉说，缥缈的梦境，宛似替声乐写的旋律一般。这种作风不但加浓了诗歌的成分，抑且加强了戏剧性。特别是他的 Adagio，往往受着德国歌谣的感应。——莫扎特的长句令人想起意大利风的歌曲（Aria）；海顿的旋律令人想起节奏空灵的法国的歌（Romance）；贝多芬的 Adagio 却充满着德国歌谣（Lied）所特有的情操：简单纯朴，亲切动人。

在贝多芬心目中，奏鸣曲典型并非不可动摇的格式，而是可以用作音乐上的辩证法的：他提出一个主句，一个副句，然后获得一个结论，结论的性质或是一方面胜利，或是两方面调和。在此我们可以获得一个理由，来说明为何贝多芬晚年特别运用赋格曲。[①]由于同一乐旨以音阶上不同的等级三四次地连续出现，由于参差不一的答句，由于这个曲体所特有的迅速而急促的演绎法，这赋格曲的风格能完满地适应作者的情绪，或者：原来孤立的一缕思想慢慢地渗透了心灵，终而至于占据全意识界；或者，凭着意志之力，精神必然而然地获得最后胜利。

总之，由于基调和主题的自由的选择，由于发展形式的改变，贝多芬把硬性的奏鸣曲典型化为表白情绪的灵活的工具。他依旧保存着乐曲的统一性，但他所重视的不在于结构或基调之统一，而在于情调和口吻（accent）之统

①　Fugue 这是巴赫以后在奏鸣曲中一向遭受摈弃的曲体。贝多芬中年时亦未采用。

一；换言之，这统一是内在的而非外在的。他是把内容来确定形式的；所以当他觉得典雅庄重的 Menuet 束缚难忍时，他根本换上了更快捷、更欢欣、更富于诙谐性、更宜于表现放肆姿态的 Scherzo。[1]当他感到原有的奏鸣曲体与他情绪的奔放相去太远时，他在题目下另加一个小标题：Quasi una Fantasia。[2]（作品第二十七号之一、之二——后者即俗称《月光曲》）

此外，贝多芬还把另一个古老的曲体改换了一副新的面目。变奏曲在古典音乐内，不过是一个主题周围加上无数的装饰而已。但在五彩缤纷的衣饰之下，本体[3]的真相始终是清清楚楚的。贝多芬却把它加以更自由的运用，[4]甚至使主体改头换面，不复可辨。有时旋律的线条依旧存在，可是节奏完全异样。有时旋律之一部被作为另一个新的乐思的起点。有时，在不断地更新的探险中，单单主题的一部分节奏或是主题的和声部分，仍和主题保持着渺茫的关系。贝多芬似乎想以一个题目为中心，把所有的音乐联想搜罗净尽。

至于贝多芬在配器法（orchestration）方面的创新，可以粗疏地归纳为三点：（一）乐队更庞大，乐器种类也更

---

[1] 按此字在意大利语中意为 joke，贝多芬原有粗犷的滑稽气氛，故在此体中的表现尤为酣畅淋漓。

[2] 意为："近于幻想曲"。

[3] 即主题。

[4] 后人称贝多芬的变奏曲为大变奏曲，以别于纯属装饰味的古典变奏曲。

多;①（二）全部乐器的更自由的运用，——必要时每种乐器可有独立的效能；②（三）因为乐队的作用更富于戏剧性，更直接表现感情，故乐队的音色不独变化迅速，且臻于前所未有的富丽之境。

在归纳他的作风时，我们不妨从两方面来说：素材③与形式④。前者极端简单，后者极端复杂，而且有不断的演变。

以一般而论，贝多芬的旋律是非常单纯的；倘若用线来表现，那是没有多少波浪，也没有多大曲折的。往往他的旋律只是音阶中的一个片段（a fragment of scale），而他最美最知名的主题即属于这一类；如果旋律上行或下行，也是用自然音音程的（diatonic interval）。所以音阶组成了旋律的骨干。他也常用完全和弦的主题和转位法（inverting）。但音阶、完全和弦、基调的基础，都是一个音乐家所能运用的最简单的元素。在旋律的主题（melodic theme）之外，他亦有交响的主题（symphonic theme）作为一个"发展"的材料，但仍是绝对的单纯：随便可举的

---

① 但庞大的程度最多不过六十八人：弦乐器五十四人，管乐、铜乐、敲击乐器十四人。这是从贝多芬手稿上——现存柏林国家图书馆——录下的数目。现代乐队演奏他的作品时，人数往往远过于此，致为批评家诟病。桑太伏阿纳有言："扩大乐队并不使作品增加伟大。"

② 以《第五交响曲》为例，Andante 里有一段，basson 占着领导地位。在 Allegro 内有一段，大提琴与 doublebasse 又当着主要角色。素不被重视的鼓，在此交响曲内的作用，尤为人所共知。

③ 包括旋律与和声。

④ 即曲体，详见本文前段分析。

例子，有《第五交响曲》最初的四音符，[1]或《第九交响曲》开端的简单的下行五度音。因为这种简单，贝多芬才能在"发展"中间保存想象的自由，尽量利用想象的富藏。而听众因无须费力就能把握且记忆基本主题，所以也能追随作者最特殊最繁多的变化。

贝多芬的和声，虽然很单纯很古典，但较诸前代又有很大的进步。不和协音的运用是更常见更自由了：在《第三交响曲》，《第八交响曲》，《告别奏鸣曲》等某些大胆的地方，曾引起当时人的毁谤（！）。他的和声最显著的特征，大抵在于转调（modulation）之自由。上面已经述及他在奏鸣曲中对基调间的关系，同一乐章内各个乐旨间的关系，并不遵守前人规律。这种情形不独见于大处，亦且见于小节。某些转调是由若干距离窎远的音符组成的，而且出之以突兀的方式，令人想起大画家所常用的"节略"手法，色彩掩盖了素描，旋律的继续被遮蔽了。

至于他的形式，因繁多与演变的迅速，往往使分析的工作难于措手。十九世纪中叶，若干史家把贝多芬的作风分成三个时期，[2]这个观点至今非常流行，但时下的批评家均嫌其武断笼统。1852 年 12 月 2 日，李斯特答复主张三期说的史家兰兹时，曾有极精辟的议论，足资我们参考，

---

① sol-sol-sol-mi^b。

② 大概是把《第三交响曲》以前的作品列为第一期，钢琴奏鸣曲至作品第二十二号为止，两部奏鸣曲至作品第三十号为止。第三至第八交响曲被列入第二期，又称为贝多芬盛年期，钢琴奏鸣曲至作品第九十号为止。作品第一百号以后至贝多芬死的作品为末期。

他说：

"对于我们音乐家，贝多芬的作品仿佛云柱与火柱，领导着以色列人在沙漠中前行，——在白天领导我们的是云柱，——在黑夜中照耀我们的是火柱，使我们夜以继日地趱奔。他的阴暗与光明同样替我们划出应走的路：它们俩都是我们永久的领导，不断的启示。倘使我要把大师在作品里表现的题旨不同的思想，加以分类的话，我决不采用现下流行①而为您采用的三期论法。我只直截了当地提出一个问题，那是音乐批评的轴心，即传统的、公认的形式，对于思想的机构的决定性，究竟到什么程度？

"用这个问题去考察贝多芬的作品，使我自然而然地把它们分作两类：第一类是传统的公认的形式包括而且控制作者的思想的；第二类是作者的思想扩张到传统形式之外，依着他的需要与灵感而把形式与风格或是破坏，或是重造，或是修改。无疑的，这种观点将使我们涉及'权威'与'自由'这两个大题目。但我们无须害怕。在美的国土内，只有天才才能建立权威，所以权威与自由的冲突，无形中消灭了，又回复了它们原始的一致，即权威与自由原是一件东西。"

这封美妙的信可以列入音乐批评史上最精彩的文章里。由于这个原则，我们可说贝多芬的一生是从事于以自由战胜传统而创造新的权威的。他所有的作品都依着这条路线进展。

---

① 系指当时。

贝多芬对整个十九世纪所发生的巨大的影响，也许至今还未告终。上一百年中面目各异的大师，门德尔松、舒曼、勃拉姆斯、李斯特、柏辽兹、瓦格纳、布鲁克纳、弗兰克，全都沾着他的雨露。谁曾想到一个父亲能有如许精神如是分歧的儿子？其缘故就因为有些作家在贝多芬身上特别关切权威这个原则，例如门德尔松与勃拉姆斯；有些则特别注意自由这个原则，例如李斯特与瓦格纳。前者努力维持古典的结构，那是贝多芬在未曾完全摒弃古典形式以前留下最美的标本的。后者，尤其是李斯特，却继承着贝多芬在交响曲方面未完成的基业，而用着大胆和深刻的精神发现交响诗的新形体。自由诗人如舒曼，从贝多芬那里学会了可以表达一切情绪的弹性的音乐语言。最后，瓦格纳不但受着《菲岱里奥》的感应，且从他的奏鸣曲、四重奏、交响曲里提炼出"连续的旋律"（mélodie continue）和"领导乐旨"（leitmotiv），把纯粹音乐搬进了乐剧的领域。

由此可见，一个世纪的事业，都是由一个人撒下种子的。固然，我们并未遗忘十八世纪的大家所给予他的粮食，例如海顿老人的主题发展，莫扎特的旋律的广大与丰满。但在时代转折之际，同时开下这许多道路，为后人树立这许多路标的，的确除贝多芬外无第二人。所以说贝多芬是古典时代与浪漫时代的过渡人物，实在是估低了他的价值，估低了他的艺术的独立性与特殊性。他的行为的光轮，照耀着整个世纪，孵育着多少不同的天才！音乐，由贝多芬从刻板严格的枷锁之下解放了出来，如今可自由地歌唱每个人的痛苦与欢乐了。由于他，音乐从死的学术一变而为活的意识。所有的来者，即使绝对不曾模仿他，即使精神与气质和他的相反，实际上也无异是他的门徒，因为他们享受着他用痛苦换来的自由！

三、重要作品浅释

为完成我这篇粗疏的研究起计，我将选择贝多芬最知名的作品加一些浅显的注解。当然，以作者的外行与浅学，既谈不到精密的技术分析，也谈不到微妙的心理解剖。我不过撷拾几个权威批评家的论见，加上我十余年来对贝多芬作品亲炙所得的观念，作一个概括的叙述而已。我的希望是，爱好音乐的人能在欣赏时有一些启蒙式的指南，在探宝山时稍有凭借；专学音乐的青年能从这些简单的引子里，悟到一件作品的内容是如何精深宏博，如何在手与眼的训练之外，需要加以深刻的体会，方能仰攀创造者的崇高的意境。——我国的音乐研究，十余年来尚未走出幼稚园；向升堂入室的路出发，现在该是时候了吧！

（一）钢琴奏鸣曲

作品第十三号：《悲怆奏鸣曲》（Sonate "Pathétique" in C min.）——这是贝多芬早年奏鸣曲中最重要的一阕，包括 Allegro—Adagio—Rondo 三章。第一章之前冠有一节悲壮严肃的引子，这一小节，以后又出现了两次：一在破题之后，发展之前；一在复题之末，结论之前。更特殊的是，副句与主句同样以小调为基础。而在小调的 Adagio 之后，Rondo 仍以小调演出。——第一章表现青年的火焰，热烈的冲动；到第二章，情潮似乎安定下来，沐浴在宁静的气氛中；但在第三章泼辣的 Rondo 内，激情重又抬头。光与暗的对照，似乎象征着悲欢的交替。

作品第二十七号之二：《**月光奏鸣曲**》［Sonate "quasi una fantasia"（"Moonlight"）in C# min.］——奏鸣曲体制在此不适用了。原应位于第二章的 Adagio，占了最重要的第一章。开首便是单调的、冗长的、缠绵无尽的独白，赤裸裸地吐露出凄凉幽怨之情。紧接着的是 Allegretto，把前章痛苦的悲吟挤逼成紧张的热情。然后是激昂迫促的 Presto，以奏鸣曲典型的体裁，如古悲剧般作一强有力的结论：心灵的力终于镇服了痛苦。情操控制着全局，充满着诗情与戏剧式的波涛，一步紧似一步。①

作品第三十一号之二：《**"暴风雨"奏鸣曲**》（Sonate "Tempest" in D min.）——1802—1803 年间，贝多芬给友人的信中说："从此我要走上一条新的路。"这支乐曲便可说是证据。音节，形式，风格，全有了新面目，全用着表情更直接的语言。第一章末戏剧式的吟诵体（récitatif），宛如庄重而激昂的歌唱。Adagio 尤其美妙，兰兹说："它令人想起韵文体的神话；受了魅惑的蔷薇，不，不是蔷薇，而是被女巫的魅力催眠的公主……"那是一片天国的平和，柔和黝黯的光明。最后的 Allegretto 则是泼辣奔放的场面，一个"仲夏夜之梦"，如罗曼·罗兰所说。

作品第五十三号：《**黎明奏鸣曲**》（Sonate l'Aurore in C）

---

① 十几年前国内就流行着一种浅薄的传说，说这曲奏鸣曲是即兴之作，而且在小说式的故事中组成的。这完全是荒诞不经之说。贝多芬作此曲时绝非出于即兴，而是经过苦心的经营而成。这有他遗下的稿本为证。

——"黎明"这个俗称，和"月光曲"一样，实在并无确切的根据。也许开始一章里的 crescendo，也许 Rondo 之前短短的 Adagio，——那种曙色初现的气氛，莱茵河上舟子的歌声，约略可以唤起"黎明"的境界。然而可以肯定的是：在此毫无贝多芬悲壮的气质，他仿佛在田野里闲步，悠然欣赏着云影、鸟语、水色，怅惘地出神着。到了 Rondo，慵懒的幻梦又转入清明高远之境。罗曼·罗兰说这支奏鸣曲是《第六交响曲》之先声，也是田园曲。①

作品第五十七号：《热情奏鸣曲》（Sonate "Appass-ionnata" in F min.）——壮烈的内心的悲剧，石破天惊的火山爆裂，莎士比亚的《暴风雨》式的气息，伟大的征服……在此我们看到了贝多芬最光荣的一次战争。——从一个乐旨上演化出来的两个主题：犷野而强有力的"我"，命令着，威镇着；战栗而怯弱的"我"，哀号着，乞求着。可是它不敢抗争，追随着前者，似乎坚忍地接受了运命，②然而精力不继，又倾倒了，在苦痛的小调上忽然停住……再起……再仆……一大段雄壮的"发展"，力的主题重又出现，滔滔滚滚地席卷着弱者，——它也不复中途蹉跌了。随后是英勇的结局（coda）。末了，主题如雷雨一般在辽远的天际消失，神秘的 pianissimo。第二章，单纯的 Andante，心灵获得须臾的休息，两片巨大的阴

---

① 通常称为田园曲的奏鸣曲，是作品第十四号；但那是除了一段乡妇的舞蹈以外，实在并无旁的田园气息。

② 一段大调的旋律。

影①中间透露一道美丽的光。然而休战的时间很短，在变奏曲之末，一切重又骚乱，吹起终局（Finale-Rondo）的旋风……在此，怯弱的"我"虽仍不时发出悲怆的呼吁，但终于被狂风暴雨②淹没了。最后的结论，无殊一片沸腾的海洋……人变了一颗原子，在吞噬一切的大自然里不复可辨。因为犷野而有力的"我"就代表着原始的自然。在第一章里犹图挣扎的弱小的"我"，此刻被贝多芬交给了原始的"力"。

作品第八十一号之 A :《告别奏鸣曲》（Sonate "Les Adieux" in E♭）③——第一乐章全部建筑在 Sol-fa-mi 三个音符之上，所有的旋律都从这简单的乐旨出发；④复题之末的结论中，告别⑤更以最初的形式反复出现。——同一主题的演变，代表着同一情操的各种区别：在引子内，"告别"是凄凉的，但是镇静的，不无甘美的意味；在 Allegro 之初，⑥它又以击撞抵触的节奏与不和协弦重现：这是匆促的分手。末了，以对白方式再三重复的"告别"几乎合为一体地以 diminuento 告终。两个朋友最后的扬巾示意，愈离愈远，消失了。——"留守"是短短的一章 Adagio，彷徨，问询，焦灼，朋友在期待中。然后是

① 第一与第三章。

② 犷野的我。

③ 本曲印行时就刊有告别、留守、重叙这三个标题。所谓告别系指奥太子鲁道夫 1809 年 5 月之远游。

④ 这一点加强了全曲情绪之统一。

⑤ 即前述的三音符。

⑥ 第一章开始时为一段迟缓的引子，然后继以 Allegro。

vivacissimamente，热烈轻快的篇章，两个朋友互相投在怀抱里。——自始至终，诗情画意笼罩着乐曲。

作品第九十号:《E小调奏鸣曲》（Sonate in E min.）——这是题赠李希诺夫斯基亲王的，他不顾家庭的反对，娶了一个女伶。贝多芬自言在这支乐曲内叙述这桩故事。第一章题作"头脑与心的交战"，第二章题作"与爱人的谈话"。故事至此告终，音乐也至此完了。而因为故事以吉庆终场，故音乐亦从小调开始，以大调结束。再以乐旨而论，在第一章内的戏剧情调和第二章内恬静的倾诉，也正好与标题相符。诗意左右着乐曲的成分，比《告别奏鸣曲》更浓厚。

作品第一〇六号:《降B大调奏鸣曲》（Sonate in B♭）——贝多芬写这支乐曲时是为了生活所迫；所以一开始便用三个粗野的和弦，展开这首惨痛绝望的诗歌。"发展"部分是头绪万端的复音配合，象征着境遇与心绪的艰窘。[①]"发展"中间两次运用赋格曲体式（Fugato）的作风，好似要寻觅一个有力的方案来解决这堆乱麻。一会儿是光明，一会儿是阴影。——随后是又古怪又粗犷的Scherzo，噩梦中的幽灵。——意志的超人的努力，引起了痛苦的反省:这是Adagio Appassionnato，慷慨的陈词，凄凉的哀吟。三个主题以大变奏曲的形式铺叙。当受难者悲恸欲绝之际，一段Largo引进了赋格曲，展开一个场面伟大、经纬错综的"发展"，运用一切对位与轮唱曲（Canon）的巧妙，来

---

① 作曲年代是1818，贝多芬正为了侄儿的事弄得焦头烂额。

陈诉心灵的苦恼。接着是一段比较宁静的插曲，预先唱出了《D调弥撒曲》内谢神的歌。——最后的结论，宣告患难已经克服，命运又被征服了一次。在贝多芬全部奏鸣曲中，悲哀的抒情成分，痛苦的反抗的吼声，从没有像在这件作品里表现得惊心动魄。

（二）提琴与钢琴奏鸣曲

在"两部奏鸣曲"中，[①]贝多芬显然没有像钢琴奏鸣曲般的成功。软性与硬性的两种乐器，他很难觅得完善的驾驭方法。而且十阕提琴与钢琴奏鸣曲内，九阕是《第三交响曲》以前所作；九阕之内五阕又是《月光奏鸣曲》以前的作品。1812年后，他不再从事于此种乐曲。在此我只介绍最特出的两曲。

作品第三十号之二：《C小调奏鸣曲》（Sonate in C min.）[②]——在本曲内，贝多芬的面目较为显著。暴烈而阴沉的主题，在提琴上演出时，钢琴在下面怒吼。副句取着威武而兴奋的姿态，兼具柔媚与遒劲的气概。终局的激昂奔放，尤其标明了贝多芬的特色。赫里欧[③]有言："如果在这件作品里去寻找胜利者[④]的雄姿与战败者的哀号，未免穿凿的话，我们至少可认为它也是英雄式的乐曲，充满

---

① 即提琴与钢琴，或大提琴与钢琴奏鸣曲。

② 题赠俄皇亚历山大二世。

③ 法国现代政治家兼音乐批评家。

④ 按系指俄皇。

着力与欢畅，堪与《第五交响曲》相比。"

作品第四十七号：《克勒策奏鸣曲》（Sonate à Kreutzer in A min.）[①]——贝多芬一向无法安排的两种乐器，在此被他找到了一个解决的途径：它们俩既不能调和，就让它们冲突；既不能携手，就让它们争斗。全曲的第一与第三乐章，不啻钢琴与提琴的肉搏。在旁的"两部奏鸣曲"中，答句往往是轻易的、典雅的美；这里对白却一步紧似一步，宛如两个仇敌的短兵相接。在 Andante 的恬静的变奏曲后，争斗重新开始，愈加紧张了，钢琴与提琴一大段急流奔泻的对位，由钢琴的洪亮的呼声结束。"发展"奔腾飞纵，忽然凝神屏息了一会儿，经过几节 Adagio，然后消没在目眩神迷的结论中间。——这是一场决斗，两种乐器的决斗，两种思想的决斗。

（三）四重奏

弦乐四重奏是以奏鸣曲典型为基础的曲体，所以在贝多芬的四重奏里，可以看到和他在奏鸣曲与交响曲内相同的演变。他的趋向是旋律的强化，发展与形式的自由；且在弦乐器上所能表现的复音配合，更为富丽，更为独立。他一共制作十六阕四重奏，但在第十一与第十二阕之间，

---

① 克勒策为法国人，为王家教堂提琴手。曾随军至维也纳，与贝多芬相遇。贝多芬遇之甚善，以此曲题赠。但克氏始终不愿演奏，因他的音乐观念迂腐守旧，根本不了解贝多芬。

相隔有十四年之久，①故最后五阕形成了贝多芬作品中一个特殊面目，显示他最后的艺术成就。当第十二阕四重奏问世之时，《D调弥撒曲》与《第九交响曲》都已诞生。他最后几年的生命是孤独、②疾病、困穷、烦恼③煎熬他最甚的时代。他慢慢地隐忍下去，一切悲苦深深地沉潜到心灵深处。他在乐艺上表现的，是更为肯定的个性。他更求深入，更爱分析，尽量汲取悲欢的灵泉，打破形式的桎梏。音乐几乎变成歌辞与语言一般，透明地传达着作者内在的情绪，以及起伏微妙的心理状态。一般人往往只知鉴赏贝多芬的交响曲与奏鸣曲；四重奏的价值，至近数十年方始被人赏识。因为这类纯粹表现内心的乐曲，必须内心生活丰富而深刻的人才能体验；而一般的音乐修养也须到相当的程度方不致在森林中迷路。

作品第一二七号:《**降 E 大调四重奏**》(Quatuor in E^b) ④——第一章里的"发展"，着重于两个原则：一是纯粹节奏的，⑤一是纯粹音阶的。⑥以静穆的徐缓的调子出现的 Adagio 包括六支连续的变奏曲，但即在节奏复杂的部分内，也仍保持默想的气息。奇谲的 Scherzo 以后的"终局"，含有多少大胆的和声，用节略手法的转调。——最

---

① 1810—1824 年。

② 尤其是艺术上的孤独，连亲近的友人都不了解他了……

③ 侄子的不长进。

④ 第十二阕。

⑤ 一个强毅的节奏与另一个柔和的节奏对比。

⑥ 两重节奏从 E^b 转到明快的 G，再转到更加明快的 C。

美妙的是那些 Adagio，[①] 好似一株树上开满着不同的花，各有各的姿态。在那些吟诵体内，时而清明，时而绝望——清明时不失激昂的情调，痛苦时并无疲倦的气色。作者在此的表情，比在钢琴上更自由；一方面传统的形式似乎依然存在，一方面给人的感应又极富于启迪性。

作品第一三〇号：《降B大调四重奏》（Quatuor in B♭）[②]——第一乐章开始时，两个主题重复演奏了四次，——两个在乐旨与节奏上都相反的主题：主句表现悲哀，副句[③]表现决心。两者的对白引入奏鸣曲典型的体制。在诙谐的 Presto 之后，接着一段插曲式的 Andante：凄凉的幻梦与温婉的惆怅，轮流控制着局面。此后是一段古老的 Menuet，予人以古风与现代风交错的韵味。然后是著名的 Cavatinte—Adagio molto espressivo，为贝多芬流着泪写的：第二小提琴似乎模仿着起伏不已的胸脯，因为它满贮着叹息；继以凄厉的悲歌，不时杂以断续的呼号……受着重创的心灵还想挣扎起来飞向光明。——这一段倘和终局作对比，就愈显得惨恻。——以全体而论，这支四重奏和以前的同样含有繁多的场面，[④]但对照更强烈，更突兀，而且全部的光线也更神秘。

作品第一三一号：《升C小调四重奏》（Quatuor in C♯

---

① 包括 Adagio ma non troppo；Andante con molto；Adagio molto espressivo。

② 第十三阕。

③ 由第二小提琴演出的。

④ Allegro 里某些句子充满着欢乐与生机，Presto 富有滑稽意味，Andante 笼罩在柔和的微光中，Menuet 借用着古德国的民歌的调子，终局则是波希米亚人放肆的欢乐。

min.）^①——开始是凄凉的 Adagio，用赋格曲写成的，浓烈的哀伤气氛，似乎预告着一篇痛苦的诗歌。瓦格纳认为这段 Adagio 是音乐上从来未有的最忧郁的篇章。然而此后的 Allegro molto vivace 却又是典雅又是奔放，尽是出人不意的快乐情调。Andante 及变奏曲，则是特别富于抒情的段落，中心感动的，微微有些不安的情绪。此后是 Presto、Adagio、Allegro，章节繁多、曲折特甚的终局。——这是一支千绪万端的大曲，轮廓分明的插曲即已有十三四支之多，仿佛作者把手头所有的材料都集合在这里了。

作品第一三二号：《A 小调四重奏》（Quatuor in A min.）^②——这是有名的"病愈者的感谢曲"。贝多芬在 Allegro 中先表现痛楚与骚乱，^③然后阴沉的天边渐渐透露光明，一段乡村舞曲代替了沉闷的冥想，一个牧童送来柔和的笛声。接着是 Allegro，四种乐器合唱着感谢神恩的颂歌。贝多芬自以为病愈了。他似乎跪在地下，合着双手。在赤裸的旋律之上（Andante），我们听见从徐缓到急促的言语，赛如大病初愈的人试着软弱的步子，逐渐回复了精力。多兴奋！多快慰！合唱的歌声再起，一次热烈一次。虔诚的情意，预示瓦格纳的《帕西法尔》歌剧。接着是 Allegro alla marcia，激发着青春的冲动。之后是终局。动作活泼，节奏明朗而均衡，但小调的旋律依旧很凄凉。病是痊愈了，创痕未曾忘记。直到旋律转入大调，低音部乐器繁杂的节

---

① 第十四阕。
② 第十五阕。
③ 第一小提琴的兴奋，和对位部分的严肃。

奏慢慢隐灭之时，贝多芬的精力才重新获得了胜利。

作品第一三五号：《**F大调四重奏**》(Quatuor in F) [1] ——这是贝多芬一生最后的作品。[2] 第一章 Allegretto 天真，巧妙，充满着幻想与爱娇，年代久远的海顿似乎复活了一刹那：最后一朵蔷薇，在萎谢之前又开放了一次。Vivace 是一篇音响的游戏，一幅纵横无碍的素描。而后是著名的 Lento，原稿上注明着"甘美的休息之歌，或和平之歌"，这是贝多芬最后的祈祷，最后的颂歌，照赫里欧的说法，是他精神的遗嘱。他那种特有的清明的心境，实在只是平复了的哀痛。单纯而肃穆，虔敬而和平的歌，可是其中仍有些急促的悲叹，最后更高远的和平之歌把它抚慰下去，——而这缕恬静的声音，不久也朦胧入梦了。终局是两个乐句剧烈争执以后的单方面的结论，乐思的奔放，和声的大胆，是这一部分的特色。

（四）协奏曲

贝多芬的钢琴与乐队合奏曲共有五支，重要的是第四与第五。提琴与乐队合奏曲共只一阕，在全部作品内不占何等地位，因为国人熟知，故亦选入。

作品第五十八号：《**G大调钢琴协奏曲**》(Concerto pour Piano et Orchestre in G) [3] ——单纯的主题先由钢琴

---

① 第十六阕。

② 未完成的稿本不计在内。

③ 第四协奏曲，1806 年作。

提出,然后继以乐队的合奏,不独诗意浓郁,抑且气势雄伟,有交响曲之格局。"发展"部分由钢琴表现出一组轻盈而大胆的面目,再以飞舞的线条(arabesque)作为结束。——但全曲最精彩的当推短短的 Andante con molto,全无技术的炫耀,只有钢琴与乐队剧烈对垒的场面。乐队奏出威严的主题,肯定是强暴的意志;胆怯的琴声,柔弱地,孤独地,用着哀求的口吻对答。对话久久继续,钢琴的呼吁越来越迫切,终于获得了胜利。全场只有它的声音,乐队好似战败的敌人般,只在远方发出隐约叫吼的回声。不久琴声也在悠然神往的和弦中缄默。——此后是终局,热闹的音响中杂有大胆的碎和声(arpeggio)。

作品第七十三号:《"帝皇"钢琴协奏曲》(Concerto "Empereur" in E^b)[1]——滚滚长流的乐句,像瀑布一般,几乎与全乐队的和弦同时揭露了这件庄严的大作。一连串的碎和音,奔腾而下,停留在 A$^#$ 的转调上。浩荡的气势,雷霆万钧的力量,富丽的抒情成分,灿烂的荣光,把作者当时的勇敢、胸襟、怀抱、骚动,[2]全部宣泄了出来。谁听了这雄壮瑰丽的第一章不联想到《第三交响曲》里的crescendo?——由弦乐低低唱起的 Adagio,庄严静穆,是一股宗教的情绪。而 Adagio 与 Finale 之间的过渡,尤令人惊叹。在终局的 Rondo 内,豪华与温情,英武与风流,又奇妙地熔冶于一炉,完成了这部大曲。

作品第六十一号:《D 大调提琴协奏曲》(Concerto

---

① 第五协奏曲,1809 年作。"帝皇"二字为后人所加的俗称。

② 1809 为拿破仑攻入维也纳之年。

pour Violon et Orchestre in D）第一章 Adagio，开首一段柔媚的乐队合奏，令人想起《第四钢琴协奏曲》的开端。两个主题的对比内，一个 C# 音的出现，在当时曾引起非难。Larghetto 的中段一个纯朴的主题唱着一支天真的歌，但奔放的热情不久替它展开了广大的场面，增加了表情的丰满。最后一章 Rondo 则是欢欣的驰骋，不时杂有柔情的倾诉。

（五）交响曲

作品第二十一号:《**第一交响曲**》（in C）①——年轻的贝多芬在引子里就用了 F 的不和协弦，与成法背驰。②虽在今日看来，全曲很简单，只有第三章的 Menuet 及其三重奏部分较为特别；以 Allegro molto vivace 奏出来的 Menuet 实际已等于 Scherzo。但当时批评界觉得刺耳的，尤其是管乐器的运用大为推广。Timbale 在莫扎特与海顿，只用来产生节奏，贝多芬却用以加强戏剧情调。利用乐器个别的音色而强调它们的对比，可说是从此奠定的基业。

作品第三十六号:《**第二交响曲**》（in D）③——制作本曲时，正是贝多芬初次的爱情失败，耳聋的痛苦开始严重地打击他的时候。然而作品的精力充溢饱满，全无颓丧之气。——引子比《第一交响曲》更有气魄：先由低音乐器演出的主题，逐渐上升，过渡到高音乐器，终于由整个

---

① 1800 年作。1800 年 4 月 2 日初次演奏。

② 照例这引子是应该肯定本曲的基调的。

③ 1801—1802 年作。1803 年 4 月 5 日演奏。

乐队合奏。这种一步紧一步的手法，以后在《第九交响曲》的开端里简直达到超人的伟大。——Larghetto 显示清明恬静、胸境宽广的意境。Scherzo 描写兴奋的对话，一方面是弦乐器，一方面是管乐和敲击乐器。终局与 Rondo 相仿，但主题之骚乱，情调之激昂，是与通常流畅的 Rondo 大相径庭的。

作品第五十五号：《第三交响曲》（《英雄交响曲》in Eᵇ）[①]——巨大的迷宫，深密的丛林，剧烈的对照，不但是音乐史上划时代的建筑，[②]抑且是空前绝后的史诗。可是当心啊，初步的听众多容易在无垠的原野中迷路！——控制全局的乐句，实在只是：

不问次要的乐句有多少，它的巍峨的影子始终矗立在天空。罗曼·罗兰把它当作一个生灵，一缕思想，一个意志，一种本能。因为我们不能把英雄的故事过于看得现实，这并非叙事或描写的音乐。拿破仑也罢，无名英雄也罢，实际只是一个因子，一个象征。真正的英雄还是贝多芬自己。第一章通篇是他双重灵魂的决斗，经过三大回合[③]方始获得一个综合的结论：钟鼓齐鸣，号角长啸，狂热的群众拥着英雄欢呼。然而其间的经过是何等曲折：多

---

① 1803 年作。1805 年 4 月 7 日初次演奏。

② 回想一下海顿和莫扎特吧。

③ 第一章内的三大段。

少次的颠扑与多少次的奋起。①这是浪与浪的冲击，巨人式的战斗！发展部分的庞大，是本曲最显著的特征，而这庞大与繁杂是适应作者当时的内心富藏的。——第二章，英雄死了！然而英雄的气息仍留在送葬者的行列间。谁不记得这幽怨而凄惶的主句：

当它在大调上时，凄凉之中还有清明之气，酷似古希腊的薤露歌。但回到小调上时，变得阴沉，凄厉，激昂，竟是莎士比亚式的悲怆与郁闷了。挽歌又发展成史诗的格局。最后，在 pianissimo 的结局中，呜咽的葬曲在痛苦的深渊内静默。——Scherzo 开始时是远方隐约的波涛似的声音，继而渐渐宏大，继而又由朦胧的号角②吹出无限神秘的调子。——终局是以富有舞曲风味的主题作成的变奏曲，仿佛是献给欢乐与自由的。但第一章的主句，英雄，重又露面，而死亡也重现了一次：可是胜利之局已定。剩下的只有光荣的结束了。

　　作品第六十号：《第四交响曲》(in B♭) ③——是贝多芬和特雷泽·布伦瑞克订婚的一年，诞生了这件可爱的、满是笑意的作品。引子从 B♭ 小调转到大调，遥远的哀伤

―――――――

① 多少次的 crescendo！

② 通常的三重奏部分。

③ 1806 年作。1807 年 3 月初次演奏。

淡忘了。活泼而有飞纵跳跃之态的主句，由大管（basson）、双簧管（hautbois）与长笛（flûte）高雅的对白构成的副句，流利自在的"发展"，所传达的尽是快乐之情。一阵模糊的鼓声，把开朗的心情微微搅动了一下，但不久又回到主题上来，以强烈的欢乐结束。——至于 Adagio 的旋律，则是徐缓的，和悦的，好似一叶扁舟在平静的水上滑过。而后是 Menuet，保存着古称而加速了节拍。号角与双簧管传达着缥缈的诗意。最后是 Allegro ma non troppo，愉快的情调重复控制全局，好似突然露脸的阳光；强烈的生机与意志，在乐队中间作了最后一次爆发。——在这首热烈的歌曲里，贝多芬泄露了他爱情的欢欣。

作品第六十七号：《**第五交响曲**》（in C min.）[①]——开首的 sol-sol-sol-mi^b 是贝多芬特别爱好的乐旨，在《第五奏鸣曲》[②]《第三四重奏》[③]《热情奏鸣曲》中，我们都曾见过它的轮廓。他曾对申德勒说："命运便是这样地来叩门的。"[④]它统率着全部乐曲。渺小的人得凭着意志之力和它肉搏，——在运命连续呼召之下，回答的永远是幽咽的问号。人挣扎着，抱着一腔的希望和毅力。但运命的口吻愈来愈威严，可怜的造物似乎战败了，只有悲叹之声。——之后，残酷的现实暂时隐灭了一下，Andante 从

---

① 俗称《命运交响曲》。1807—1808 年间作。1808 年 12 月 22 日初次演奏。

② 作品第九号之一。

③ 作品第十八号之三。

④ 命运二字的俗称即渊源于此。

深远的梦境内传来一支和平的旋律。胜利的主题出现了三次。接着是行军的节奏，清楚而又坚定，扫荡了一切矛盾。希望抬头了，屈服的人恢复了自信。然而 Scherzo 使我们重新下地去面对阴影。运命再现，可是被粗野的舞曲与诙谐的 staccati 和 pizziccati 挡住。突然，一片黑暗，唯有隐约的鼓声，乐队延续奏着七度音程的和弦，然后迅速的 crescendo 唱起凯旋的调子。[①]运命虽再呼喊，[②]不过如噩梦的回忆，片刻即逝。胜利之歌再接再厉地响亮。意志之歌切实宣告了终篇。——在全部交响曲中，这是结构最谨严，部分最均衡，内容最凝练的一阕。批评家说："从未有人以这么少的材料表达过这么多的意思。"

作品第六十八号：《**第六交响曲**》(《田园交响曲》in F）[③]——这阕交响曲是献给自然的。原稿上写着："纪念乡居生活的田园交响曲，注重情操的表现而非绘画式的描写。"由此可见作者在本曲内并不想模仿外界，而是表现一组印象。——第一章 Allegro，题为"下乡时快乐的印象"。在提琴上奏出的主句，轻快而天真，似乎从斯拉夫民歌上采来的。这个主题的冗长的"发展"，始终保持着深邃的平和，恬静的节奏，平衡的转调；全无次要乐曲的羼入。同样的乐旨和面目来回不已。这是一个人面对着一幅固定的图画悠然神往的印象。——第二章

---

① 这时已经到了终局。

② Scherzo 的主题又出现了一下。

③ 1807—1808 年间作。1808 年 12 月 22 日初次演奏。

Andante,"溪畔小景",中音弦乐,①象征着潺潺的流水,是"逝者如斯,往者如彼,而盈虚者未尝往也"的意境。林间传出夜莺②、鹌鹑③、杜鹃④的啼声,合成一组三重奏。——第三章 Scherzo,"乡人快乐的宴会"。先是三拍子的华尔兹,——乡村舞曲,继以二拍子的粗野的蒲雷舞。⑤突然远处一种隐雷,⑥一阵静默……几道闪电。⑦俄而是暴雨和霹雳一齐发作。然后雨散云收,青天随着 C 大调的上行音阶⑧重新显现。——而后是第四章 Allegretto,"牧歌,雷雨之后的快慰与感激"。——一切重归宁谧:潮湿的草原上发出清香,牧人们歌唱,互相应答,整个乐曲在平和与喜悦的空气中告终。——贝多芬在此忘记了忧患,心上反映着自然界的甘美与闲适,抱着泛神的观念,颂赞着田野和农夫牧子。

作品第九十二号:《第七交响曲》(in A)⑨——开首一大段引子,平静的,庄严的,气势是向上的,但是有节度的。多少的和弦似乎推动着作品前进。用长笛奏出的主题,展开了第一乐章的中心:Vivace。活跃的节奏控制着全曲,所有的音域,所有的乐器,都由它来支配。这儿分

---

① 第二小提琴,次高音提琴,两架大提琴。

② 长笛表现。

③ 双簧管表现。

④ 单簧管表现。

⑤ 法国一种地方舞。

⑥ 低音弦乐。

⑦ 小提琴上短短的碎和音。

⑧ 还有笛音点缀。

⑨ 1812 年作。1813 年 12 月 8 日初次演奏。

不出主句或副句；参加着奔腾飞舞的运动的，可说有上百的乐旨，也可说只有一个。——Allegretto 却把我们突然带到另一个世界。基本主题和另一个忧郁的主题轮流出现，传出苦痛和失望之情。——然后是第三章，在戏剧化的 Scherzo 以后，紧接着美妙的三重奏，似乎均衡又恢复了一刹那。终局则是快乐的醉意，急促的节奏，再加一个粗犷的旋律，最后达于 crescendo 这紧张狂乱的高潮。——这支乐曲的特点是：一些单纯而显著的节奏产生出无数的乐旨；而其兴奋动乱的气氛，恰如瓦格纳所说的，有如"祭献舞神"的乐曲。

作品第九十三号：《第八交响曲》（in F）[①]——在贝多芬的交响曲内，这是一支小型的作品，宣泄着兴高采烈的心情。短短的 Allegro，纯是明快的喜悦、和谐而自在的游戏。——在 Scherzo 部分[②]，作者故意采用过时的 Menuet，来表现端庄娴雅的古典美。——到了终局的 Allegro vivace 则通篇充满着笑声与平民的幽默。有人说，是"笑"产生这部作品的。我们在此可发现贝多芬的另一副面目，像儿童一般，他做着音响的游戏。

作品第一二五号：《第九交响曲》（《合唱交响曲》，Choral Symphony in D min.）[③]——《第八》之后十一年的作品，贝多芬把他过去在音乐方面的成就作了一个综合，

---

① 1812 年作。1814 年 2 月 27 日初次演奏。

② 第三章内。

③ 1822—1824 年间作。1824 年 5 月 7 日初次演奏。

同时走上了一条新路。——乐曲开始时，①la-mi 的和音，好似从远方传来的呻吟，也好似从深渊中浮起来的神秘的形象，直到第十七节，才响亮地停留在 D 小调的基调上。而后是许多次要的乐旨，而后是本章的副句②……《第二》《第五》《第六》《第七》《第八》各交响曲里的原子，迅速地露了一下脸，回溯着他一生的经历，把贝多芬完全笼盖住的阴影，在作品中间移过。现实的命运重新出现在他脑海里。巨大而阴郁的画面上，只有若干简短的插曲映入些微光明。——第二章 Molto vivace，实在便是 Scherzo。句读分明的节奏，在《弥撒曲》和《菲岱里奥序曲》内都曾应用过，表示欢畅的喜悦。在中段，单簧管与双簧管引进一支细腻的牧歌，慢慢地传递给整个的乐队，使全章都蒙上明亮的色彩。——第三章 Adagio 似乎使心灵远离了一下现实。短短的引子只是一个梦。接着便是庄严的旋律，虔诚的祷告逐渐感染了热诚与平和的情调。另一旋律又出现了，凄凉的，惆怅的。然后远处吹起号角，令你想起人生的战斗。可是热诚与平和未曾消灭，最后几节的 pianissimo 把我们留在甘美的凝想中。——但幻梦终于像水泡似的隐灭了，终局最初七节的 Presto 又卷起激情与冲突的旋涡。全曲的元素一个一个再现，全溶解在此最后一章内。③从此起，贝多芬在调整你的情绪，准备接受随后

---

① Allegro ma non troppo.

② B♭ 大调。

③ 先是第一章的神秘的影子，继而是 Scherzo 的主题，Adagio 的乐旨，但都被 doublebasse 上吟诵体的问句阻住去路。

的合唱了。大提琴为首，渐渐领着全乐队唱起美妙的精纯的乐句，铺陈了很久；于是旷野的引子又领出那句吟诵体，但如今非复最低音提琴，而是男中音的歌唱了："噢，朋友，无须这些声音，且来听更美更愉快的歌声。"[①]——接着，乐队与合唱同时唱起《欢乐颂》的"欢乐，神明的美丽的火花，天国的女儿……"——每节诗在合唱之前，先由乐队传出诗的意境。合唱是由四个独唱员和四部男女合唱组成的。欢乐的节会由远而近，然后大众唱着："拥抱啊，千千万万的生灵……"当乐曲终了之时，乐器的演奏者和歌唱员赛似两条巨大的河流，汇合成一片音响的海。——在贝多芬的意念中，欢乐是神明在人间的化身，它的使命是把习俗和刀剑分隔的人群重行结合。它的口号是友谊与博爱。它的象征是酒，是予人精力的旨酒。由于欢乐，我们方始成为不朽。所以要对天上的神明致敬，对使我们入于更苦之域的痛苦致敬。在分裂的世界之上，——一个以爱为本的神。在分裂的人群之中，欢乐是唯一的现实。爱与欢乐合为一体。这是柏拉图式的又是基督教式的爱。——除此以外，席勒的《欢乐颂》，在十九世纪初期对青年界有着特殊的影响。[②]第一是诗中的民主与共和色彩在德国自由思想者的心目中，无殊《马赛曲》之于法国人。无疑地，这也是贝多芬的感应之一。其次，席勒诗中颂扬着欢乐、友爱、夫妇之爱，都是贝多芬一生渴望而未能实现的，所以尤有共鸣作用。——最后，我们更当注意，贝多芬在

---

① 这是贝多芬自作的歌词，不在席勒原作之内。

② 贝多芬属意于此诗篇，前后共有二十年之久。

此把字句放在次要地位；他的用意是要使器乐和人声打成一片，——而这人声既是他的，又是我们大众的，——使音乐从此和我们的心融合为一，好似血肉一般不可分离。

（六）宗教音乐

作品第一二三号：《D调弥撒曲》（Missa Solemnis in D）——这件作品始于 1817 年，成于 1823 年。当初是为奥皇太子鲁道夫兼任大主教的典礼写的，结果非但失去了时效，作品的重要也远远地超过了酬应的性质。贝多芬自己说这是他一生最完满的作品。——以他的宗教观而论，虽然生长在基督旧教的家庭里，他的信念可不完全合于基督教义。他心目之中的上帝是富有人间气息的。他相信精神不死须要凭着战斗、受苦与创造，和纯以皈依、服从、忏悔为主的基督教哲学相去甚远。在这一点上他与米开朗琪罗有些相似。他把人间与教会的篱垣撤去了，他要证明"音乐是比一切智慧与哲学更高的启示"。在写作这件作品时，他又说："从我的心里流出来，流到大众的心里。"

全曲依照弥撒祭曲礼的程序，①分成五大颂曲：（一）吾主怜我（Kyrie）；（二）荣耀归主（Gloria）；（三）我信我主（Credo）；（四）圣哉圣哉（Sanctus）；（五）神之羔

①　按弥撒祭歌唱的词句，皆有经文——拉丁文的——规定，任何人不能更易一字，各段文字大同小异，而节目繁多，谱为音乐时部门尤为庞杂。凡不解经典及不知典礼的人较难领会。

羊（Agnus Dei）。[1]——第一部以热诚的祈祷开始，继以Andante奏出"怜我怜我"的悲叹之声，对基督的呼吁，在各部合唱上轮流唱出。[2]——第二部表示人类俯伏卑恭，颂赞上帝，歌颂主荣，感谢恩赐。——第三部，贝多芬流露出独有的口吻了。开始时的庄严巨大的主题，表现他坚决的信心。结实的节奏，特殊的色彩，trompette 的运用，作者把全部乐器的机能用来证实他的意念。他的神是胜利的英雄，是半世纪后尼采所宣扬的"力"的神。贝多芬在耶稣的苦难上发现了他自身的苦难。在受难、下葬等壮烈悲哀的曲调以后，接着是复活的呼声，英雄的神明胜利了！——第四部，贝多芬参见了神明，从天国回到人间，散布一片温柔的情绪。然后如《第九交响曲》一般，是欢乐与轻快的爆发。紧接着祈祷，苍茫的，神秘的。虔诚的信徒匍匐着，已经蒙到主的眷顾。——第五部，他又代表着遭劫的人类祈求着"神之羔羊"，祈求"内的和平与外的和平"，像他自己所说。

（七）其他

作品第一三八号之三：《雷奥诺序曲第三》（Ouverture

---

[1]　全曲以四部独唱与管弦乐队及大风琴演出。乐队的构成如下：2 flûtes；2 hautbois；2 clarinettes；2 bassons；1 contrebasse；4 cors（horns）；2 trompettes；2 trombones；timbale 外加弦乐五重奏，人数之少非令人想象所及。

[2]　五大部每部皆如奏鸣曲式分成数章，兹不详解。

de Leonore No.3）[①]——脚本出于一极平庸的作家，贝多芬所根据的乃是原作的德译本。事述西班牙人弗洛雷斯当向法官唐·法尔南控告毕萨尔之罪，而反被诬陷，蒙冤下狱。弗妻雷奥诺化名菲岱里奥[②]入狱救援，终获释放。故此剧初演时，戏名下另加小标题："一名夫妇之爱"。——序曲开始时（Adagio），为弗洛雷斯当忧伤的怨叹。继而引入Allegro。在 trompette 宣告释放的信号[③]之后，雷奥诺与弗洛雷斯当先后表示希望、感激、快慰等各阶段的情绪。结束一节，尤暗示全剧明快的空气。

在贝多芬之前，格鲁克与莫扎特，固已在序曲与歌剧之间建立密切的关系；但把戏剧的性格、发展的路线归纳起来，而把序曲构成交响曲式的作品，确从《雷奥诺》开

---

① 贝多芬完全的歌剧只此一出。但从 1803 起到他死为止，二十四年间他一直断断续续地为这件作品花费着心血。1805 年 11 月初次在维也纳上演时，剧名叫作《菲岱里奥》，演出的结果很坏。1806 年 3 月，经过修改后，换了《雷奥诺》的名字再度出演，仍未获得成功。1814 年 5 月，又经一次大修改，仍用《菲岱里奥》之名上演。从此，本剧才算正式被列入剧院的戏目里。但 1827 年，贝多芬去世前数星期，还对朋友说他有一部《菲岱里奥》的手稿压在纸堆下。可知他在 1814 年以后仍在修改。现存的《菲岱里奥》，共只二幕，为 1814 年稿本，目前戏院已不常贴演。在音乐会中不时可以听到的，只是片段的歌唱。至今仍为世人熟知的，乃是它的序曲。——因为名字屡次更易，故序曲与歌剧之名今日已不统一。普通于序曲多称《雷奥诺》，于歌剧多称《菲岱里奥》；但亦不一定如此。再本剧序曲共有四支，以后贝多芬每改一次，即另作一次序曲。至今最著名的为第三序曲。

② 西班牙文，意为忠贞。

③ 法官登场一场。

始。以后韦伯、舒曼、瓦格纳等在歌剧方面，李斯特在交响诗方面，皆受到极大的影响，称《雷奥诺》为"近世抒情剧之父"。它在乐剧史上的重要，正不下于《第五交响曲》之于交响乐史。

附　录：

（一）贝多芬另有两支迄今知名的序曲：一是《科里奥兰序曲》(Ouverture de Coriolan), [①] 把两个主题作成强有力的对比：一方面是母亲的哀求，一方面是儿子的固执。同时描写这顽强的英雄在内心里的争斗。——另一支是《哀格蒙特序曲》(Ouverture d'Egmont), [②] 描写一个英雄与一个民族为自由而争战，而高歌胜利。

（二）在贝多芬所作的声乐内，当以歌（Lied）为最著名。如《悲哀的快感》，传达亲切深刻的诗意；如《吻》充满着幽默；如《鹌鹑之歌》，纯是写景之作。——至于《弥侬》[③] 的热烈的情调，尤与诗人原作吻合。此外尚有《致久别的爱人》[④]，

---

① 作品第六十二号。根据莎士比亚的本事，述一罗马英雄名科里奥兰者，因不得民众欢心，愤而率领异族攻略罗马，及抵城下，母妻遮道泣谏，卒以罢兵。

② 作品第八十五号。根据歌德的悲剧，述十六世纪荷兰贵族哀格蒙特伯爵，领导民众反抗西班牙统治之史实。

③ 歌德原作。

④ 作品第九十八号。

四部合唱的《挽歌》①，与以歌德的诗谱成的《平静的海》与《快乐的旅行》等，均为知名之作。

1943 年作

---

① 作品第一一八号。

图书在版编目（CIP）数据

　贝多芬传：汉英对照 ／（法）罗曼·罗兰著；傅雷
译 . —南京：译林出版社，2024.5
　（双语经典）
　ISBN 978-7-5753-0044-5

　I.①贝… II.①罗… ②傅… III.①英语 – 汉语 –
对照读物　IV.① H319.4

　中国国家版本馆 CIP 数据核字（2024）第 043737 号

贝多芬传　〔法国〕罗曼·罗兰／著　傅　雷／译

责任编辑　陈绍敏
特约编辑　张艳华　苏雪莹
装帧设计　鹏飞艺术
校　　对　刘文硕
责任印制　贺　伟

出版发行　译林出版社
地　　址　南京市湖南路 1 号 A 楼
邮　　箱　yilin@yilin.com
网　　址　www.yilin.com
市场热线　010-85376701
排　　版　鹏飞艺术
印　　刷　三河市中晟雅豪印务有限公司
开　　本　889 毫米 ×1194 毫米　1/32
印　　张　8.75
版　　次　2024 年 5 月第 1 版
印　　次　2024 年 5 月第 1 次印刷
书　　号　ISBN 978-7-5753-0044-5
定　　价　39.80元

BEETHOVEN

Romain Rolland

Translated by B. Constance Hull

CONTENTS

PREFACE[①]

"I want to prove that whoever acts rightly and
nobly, can by that alone bear misfortune."

BEETHOVEN

(To the Municipality of Vienna, Feb. 1, 1819.)

The air is heavy around us. The world is stifled by a thick and vitiated atmosphere—an undignified materialism which weighs on the mind and heart hindering the work of governments and individuals alike. We are being suffocated. Let us throw open the windows that God's free air may come in, and that we may breathe the breath of heroes.

Life is stern. It is a daily battle for those not content with an unattractive mediocrity of soul. And a sad battle it is, too, for many—a combat without grandeur, without happiness, fought in solitude and silence. Weighed down by poverty and domestic cares, by excessive and senseless tasks which waste the

---

① 编注：对应中译本的"初版序"。

strength to no purpose, without a gleam of hope, many souls are separated from each other, without even the consolation of holding out a hand to their brothers in misfortune who ignore them and are ignored by them. They are forced to rely on themselves alone; and there are moments when even the strongest give way under their burden of trouble. They call out—for a friend.

Let them then gather around themselves the heroic friends of the past—the great souls who suffered for the good of universal humanity. The lives of great men are not written for the proud or for the ambitious; they are dedicated rather to the unhappy. And who really is not? To those who suffer, we offer the balm of their sacred sufferings. No one is alone in the fight. The darkness of the world is made clear by the guiding light of the souls of the heroes.

I do not give the name hero to those who have triumphed by infinite thought or by sheer physical strength—but only to those made great by goodness of heart. Beethoven wrote, "I recognise no sign of superiority in mankind other than goodness." Where the character is not great, there is no great man, there is not even a great artist, nor a great man of action; there are only idols unearthed for the cheap and short-lived applause of the multitude; time will efface them altogether. Outward success matters little. The only thing is to be great, not to appear so.

The lives of the great heroes were lives of one long

martyrdom; a tragic destiny willed their souls to be forged on the anvil of physical and moral grief, of misery and ill-health. They were made great through their misfortune. Because these mighty souls complained little of their unhappiness, the best of humanity is with them. Let us gather courage from them; for torrents of quiet strength and inspiring goodness issued from their great hearts. Without even consulting their works or hearing their voices, we read in their eyes the secret of their lives—that it is good to have been in trouble, for thence the character acquires even more greatness, happiness and fruition.

The strong and pure Beethoven himself hoped in the midst of his sufferings that his example would give help to other unfortunate ones... "that the unhappy being may be consoled in finding another as unfortunate as himself, who in face of all obstacles has done everything possible to become worthy of the name, MAN." After years of battling with almost superhuman efforts to rise superior to his sufferings and accomplish his life's work—to breathe a little more courage into poor weak humanity, this conquering Prometheus observed to a friend who called too much on God, "O man, help thyself!"

May we be inspired by his noble words. Animated by the example of this man's faith in life and his quiet confidence in himself, let us again take heart.

ROMAIN ROLLAND.

HIS LIFE[1]

BEETHOVEN AT THE AGE OF 21.

From a Miniature by Gerhard von Kügelgen.

---

[1] 编注：因该英译本与傅雷先生的中译本均译自法文，译者理解有别，故中英译本之间有少量不完全对应之处。

Woltuen, wo man kann
Freiheit über alles lieben,
Wahrheit nie, auch sogar am
Throne nicht verleugnen.

Beethoven
(Album-leaf, 1792)

To do all the good one can,
To love liberty above everything,
And even if it be for a kingdom,
Never to betray truth.

He was short and thick set, broad shouldered and of athletic build. A big face, ruddy in complexion—except towards the end of his life, when his colour became sickly and yellow, especially in the winter after he had been remaining indoors far from the fields. He had a massive and rugged forehead, extremely black and extraordinarily thick hair through which it seemed the comb had never passed, for it was always very rumpled, veritable bristling "serpents of Medusa." [1] His eyes shone with prodigious force. It was one of the chief things one noticed on first encountering him, but many were mistaken in their colour. When they shone out in dark splendour from a sad and tragic visage, they generally appeared black; but they

_____

[1]   J. Russell (1822). Charles Czerny who, when a child, saw him in 1801 with a beard of several days' growth, hair bristling, wearing a waistcoat and trousers of goats' wool, thought he had met Robinson Crusoe.

were really a bluish grey.[1] Small and very deep-set, they flashed fiercely in moments of passion or warmth, and dilated in a peculiar way under the influence of inspiration, reflecting his thoughts with a marvellous exactness.[2] Often they inclined upwards with a melancholy expression. His nose was short and broad with the nostrils of a lion; the mouth refined, with the lower lip somewhat prominent. He had very strong jaws, which would easily break nuts, a large indentation in his chin imparted a curious irregularity to the face. "He had a charming smile," said Moscheles, "and in conversation a manner often lovable and inviting confidence; on the other hand his laugh was most disagreeable, loud, discordant and strident"—the laugh of a man unused to happiness. His usual expression was one of melancholy. Rellstab in 1825 said that he had to summon up all his courage to prevent himself from breaking into tears when he looked into Beethoven's "tender eyes with their speaking sadness." Braun von Braunthal met him in an inn a year later. Beethoven was sitting in a corner with closed eyes, smoking a long pipe—a habit which grew on him more and more as he approached death. A friend spoke to him. He smiled sadly, drew from his pocket a little note-tablet, and in a thin voice

[1] The painter Kloeber's remark, when he painted his portrait about 1818.

[2] Dr. W. C. Müller observed particularly "his fine eloquent eyes sometimes so kind and tender, at other times so wild, threatening and awe inspiring" (1820).

which frequently sounded cracked notes, asked him to write down his request. His face would frequently become suddenly transfigured, maybe in the access of sudden inspiration which seized him at random, even in the street, filling the passers-by with amazement, or it might be when great thoughts came to him suddenly, when seated at the piano. "The muscles of his face would stand out, his veins would swell; his wild eyes would become doubly terrible. His lips trembled, he had the manner of a wizard controlling the demons which he had invoked." "...A Shakespearean visage—'King Lear'"[1]—so Sir Julius Benedict described it.

Ludwig van Beethoven was born on December 16th, 1770, in a little bare attic of a humble dwelling at Bonn, a small University town on the Rhine near Cologne. He came of Flemish origin.[2] His father was an illiterate and lazy tenor singer—a "good-for-nothing fellow" and a confirmed drunkard. His mother was the daughter of a cook. She had been a

---

[1]   Kloeber said "Ossian's." All these details are taken from notes of Beethoven's friends, or from travellers who saw him, such as Czerny, Moscheles, Kloeber, Daniel Amadeus Atterbohm, W. C. Müller, J. Russel, Julius Benedict, Rochlitz, etc.

[2]   His grandfather, Ludwig, the most remarkable man of the family and whom Beethoven most resembled, was born at Antwerp, and only settled at Bonn in his twentieth year when he became choir master to the Prince Elector. We must not forget this fact to understand properly the passionate independence of Beethoven's nature and so many other traits which are not really German in his character.

maidservant and by her first marriage was the widow of *a valet de chambre.*

Unlike the more fortunate Mozart, Beethoven spent an unhappy childhood devoid of domestic comfort. From his earliest years life was for him a sad, even a brutal, fight for existence. His father wished to exploit the boy's musical talents and to turn him to lucrative purposes as a prodigy. At the age of four he compelled the boy to practise on the harpsichord for hours together and he shut him up alone with the violin, forcing him to work in this way. It is astonishing that the boy was not completely disgusted with music, for the father persisted in this treatment for many years, often resorting to actual violence. Beethoven's youth was saddened by the care and anxiety of earning his daily bread by tasks far too burdensome for his age. When he was eleven years old he was placed in the theatre orchestra; at thirteen he became an organist of the chapel. In 1787 he lost his mother whom he adored. "She was so good to me, so worthy of love, the best friend I had! How happy was I when I could utter that dear name of mother and she could hear it!" [1] She died of consumption and Beethoven believed himself to be affected with the same complaint. Already he suffered continually, and a depression of spirits even more terrible than the physical pain hung over him always. [2] When

---

[1] Letter to Dr. Schade at Augsburg, 15th September, 1787.
[2] Later on, in 1816, he said: "He is a poor man who does not know how to die! I myself knew, when I was but fifteen."

Thirteen-year-old Beethoven, 1783

he was seventeen he was practically the head of the family and responsible for the education of his two younger brothers. He suffered the humiliation of being obliged to beg for a pension for his father, that his father's pension should be paid to himself, as the father only squandered it in drink. These sad experiences made a profound impression on the youth. However, he found great affection and sympathy from a family in Bonn who always remained very dear to him—the Breuning family. The gentle "Lorchen," Eleonore von Breuning, was two years younger than Beethoven. He taught her music and she initiated him into the charms of poetry. She was the companion of his youth and there may have been between them a still more tender sentiment. Later on Eleonore married Dr. Wegeler, one of Beethoven's best friends; and up to Beethoven's last day there existed between the three a deep, steady friendship, amply proven by the regular and loving epistles of Wegeler and Eleonore, and those of their old faithful friend (*alter treuer Freund*) to the dear good Wegeler (*guter lieber Wegeler*). These friendly bonds became all the more touching as old age crept on all three, and still their hearts remained warm. [1] Beethoven also found a safe guide and good friend in Christian Gottlob Neefe, his music master, whose high moral character had no less influence on the young musician than did his broad and his

---

[1] We quote from several of these letters in a later part of the book, pages 65, *et seq*.

intelligent, artistic views.

Sad as was the childhood of Beethoven, he always treasured a tender and melancholy memory of the places where it was spent. Though compelled to leave Bonn, and destined to spend nearly the whole of his life in the frivolous city of Vienna with its dull environs, he never forgot the beautiful Rhine valley and the majestic river. "*Unser Vater Rhine*" (our father Rhine) as he called it, was to him almost human in its sympathy, being like some gigantic soul whose deep thoughts are beyond all human reckoning. No part is more beautiful, more powerful, more calm, than that part where the river caresses the shady and flowered slopes of the old University city of Bonn. There Beethoven spent the first twenty years of his life. There the dreams of his waking heart were born—in the fields, which slope languishingly down to the water side, with their mist-capped poplars, their bushes and their willows and the fruit trees whose roots are steeped in the rapid silent stream. And all along lying gently on the banks, strangely soft, are towns, churches, and even cemeteries, whilst away on the horizon the blue tints of the Seven Mountains show in wild jagged edges against the sky, forming a striking background to the graceful, slender, dream-like silhouettes of old ruined castles. His heart remained ever faithful to the beautiful, natural surroundings of his childhood, and until his very last moment he dreamt of seeing these scenes once again. "My native land, the beautiful country where I first saw the light of day; it is always as clear and as beautiful in my eyes as when I left it."[1] He never saw it again.

In November, 1792, Beethoven removed to Vienna, the musical metropolis of Germany.[2] The Revolution had broken out. It threatened to spread over the whole of Europe. Beethoven left Bonn just at the moment when the war reached it. On his way to Vienna he passed the Hessian armies marching to France. In 1796 and 1797 he set the war poems of Friedberg to music: a Song of Farewell, and a patriotic chorus; *Ein grosses deutsches Volk sind wir* (A great German people are we). But it was in vain that he sang of the enemies of the Revolution; the Revolution overcame the world—and Beethoven with it. From 1798, in spite of the strained relations between Austria and France, Beethoven became closely connected with the French, with the Embassy and General Bernadotte, who had just arrived in Vienna. In this intercourse strong republican sympathies showed themselves in Beethoven, and these feelings became stronger and stronger with time.

A sketch which Steinhauser made of him at this time

---

[1] To Wegeler, 29th June, 1801.

[2] He had already made a short stay there, in the spring of 1787. On that occasion he met Mozart who, however, took little notice of him. Haydn, whose acquaintance he made at Bonn in December, 1790, gave him some lessons. Beethoven also had for masters, Albrechtsberger and Salieri. The firstnamed taught him Counterpoint and Fugue, the second trained him in vocal writing.

gives a good idea of his general appearance at this period. This portrait of Beethoven is to later ones what Guérin's portrait of Napoleon is to the other effigies. Guérin's face is rugged, almost savage, and wasted with ambition. Beethoven looks very young for his age, thin and straight, very stiff in his high cravat, a defiant, strained look in his eyes; he knows his own worth and is confident of his power. In 1796 he wrote in his notebook, "Courage! in spite of all my bodily weakness my genius shall yet triumph.... Twenty-five years! that is my age now.... This very year the man I am, must reveal himself entirely." [1] Both Madame von Bernhard and Gelinck say that he was extremely proud with rough and clumsy ways and spoke with a strong provincial accent. Only his intimate friends knew what exquisite talent lay hidden under this rough exterior. Writing to Wegeler about his successes, the first thought that springs to his mind is the following: "for example, I meet a friend in need; if my purse does not allow me to help him at once, I have only to go to my work table, and in a short time I have removed his trouble.... See how charming it is to do this." [2] And a little further on, he says: "My art shall be devoted to no other object than the relief of the poor" (*Dann soll meine Kunst sich nur zum Besten der Armen zeigen*).

---

[1]   It can hardly be called his début, for his first Concert in Vienna had taken place on 30th March, 1795.

[2]   To Wegeler, 29th June, 1801 (Nohl 14). "None of my friends shall want whilst I have anything," he wrote to Ries about 1801.

Trouble was already knocking at the door; it entered—never more to leave him. Between 1796 and 1800, deafness began its sad work. He suffered from continual singing and humming in his ears. [1] His hearing became gradually weaker. For several years he kept the secret to himself, even from his dearest friends. He avoided company, so that his infliction should not be noticed. But in 1801 he can no longer remain silent; and in his despair he confides in two of his friends, Dr. Wegeler and Pastor Amenda.

"My dear, good, loving Amenda, how often have I longed

---

[1]   In his Will and Testament of 1802, Beethoven says that his deafness first appeared six years before—very likely in 1796. Let us notice in passing that in the catalogue of his works, Opus one alone (Three Trios) was written before 1796. Opus 2, the first three Piano Sonatas appeared in March, 1796. It may, therefore, be said that nearly the whole of Beethoven's work is that of a deaf man.

See the article on Beethoven's deafness by Dr. Klotz Forest in the "Medical Chronicle" of 15th May, 1905. The writer of the article believes that the complaint had its origin in a general hereditary affliction (perhaps in the phthisis of his mother). The deafness increased without ever becoming total. Beethoven heard low sounds better than high ones. In his last years it is said that he used a wooden rod, one end of which was placed in the piano sound-box, the other between his teeth. He used this means of hearing when he composed.

(On the same question see C. G. Cunn: *Wiener medizinische Wochenschrift*, February-March, 1892; Nagel: *Die Musik* (15th March, 1902); Theodor von Frimmel: *Der Merker*, July, 1912).

There are preserved in the Beethoven museum at Bonn the acoustical instruments made for Beethoven, about 1814, by the mechanician Maelzel.

Drawing by Carl Traugott Riedel, 1801

to have you near me! Your Beethoven is very unhappy. You must know that the best part of me, my hearing, has become very weak. Even at the time when we were together I was aware of distressing symptoms which I kept to myself; but my condition is now much worse.... Can I ever be cured? Naturally I hope so; but my hopes are very faint, for such maladies are the least hopeful of all. How sad my life is! For I am obliged to avoid all those I love and all that are dear to me; and all this in a world so miserable and so selfish!... How sad is this resignation in which I take refuge! Of course I have steeled myself to rise above all these misfortunes. But how is this going to be possible? [1] ..."

And to Wegeler: "...I lead a miserable life indeed. For the last two years I have completely avoided all society, for I cannot talk with my fellow-men. I am deaf. Had my profession been any other, things might still be bearable; but as it is, my situation is terrible. What will my enemies say? And they are not few!... At the theatre I always have to be quite near the orchestra in order to understand the actor. I cannot hear the high notes of the instruments or the voices, if I am but a little distance off.... When anyone speaks quietly I only hear with difficulty,... On the other hand, I find it unbearable when people shout to me.... Often I have cursed my very existence. Plutarch has

---

[1] I have translated these extracts from M. Rolland's text. Mr. Shedlock's translation from the original German may be seen on pages 65 *et seq.*—B.C.H.

guided me to a spirit of resignation. If it be possible at all, I will courageously bear with my fate; but there are moments in my life when I feel the most miserable of all God's creatures.... Resignation! What a sorry refuge! And yet it is the only one left to me!"

This tragic sadness is expressed in some of the works of this period, in the *Sonate pathétique* Op. 13 (1799), and especially in the *Largo* of the Piano Sonata in D, Opus 10, No. 3 (1798). It is a marvel that we do not find it in all the works; the radiant *Septet* (1800), the limpid *First Symphony* (C Major, 1800), both breathe a spirit of youthful gaiety. There is no doubt that he is determined to accustom his soul to grief. The spirit of man has such a strong desire for happiness that when it has it not, it is forced to create it. When the present has become too painful, the soul lives on the past. Happy days are not effaced at one stroke. Their radiance persists long after they have gone. Alone and unhappy in Vienna, Beethoven took refuge in the remembrances of his native land; his thoughts were always of Bonn. The theme of the *Andante* for the Variation in the *Septet* is a Rhenish Song. The Symphony in C Major is also inspired by the Rhine. It is a poem of youth smiling over its own dreams. It is gay and languorous; one feels there the hope and the desire of pleasing. But in certain passages in the Introduction, in the shading of the sombre bass passages of the *Allegro*, in this young composer, in the fantastic *Scherzo*, one feels with emotion the promise of the great genius to come. The expression calls to mind the eyes of Botticelli's *Bambino* in his *Holy Families*—those eyes of a little child in which one already divines the approaching tragedy.

Troubles of another kind were soon to be added to his physical sufferings. Wegeler says that he never knew Beethoven to be free of a love passion carried to extremes. These love affairs seemed to have always been of the purest kind. With him there was no connection between passion and pleasure. The confusion established between the two things nowadays only shows how little most men know of passion and its extreme rarity. Beethoven had something of the Puritan in his nature; licentious conversation and thoughts were abhorrent to him; he had always unchangeable ideas on the sanctity of love.... It is said that he could not forgive Mozart for having prostituted his genius by writing *Don Giovanni*. Schindler, who was his intimate friend, assures us that "he spent his life in virginal modesty without ever having to reproach himself for any weakness." Such a man was destined to be the dupe and victim of love; and so indeed it came about. He was always falling violently in love and ceaselessly dreaming of its happiness, only however to be deceived and to be plunged in the deepest suffering. In these alternating states of love and passionate grief, of youthful confidence and outraged pride, we find the most fruitful source of Beethoven's inspiration, until at length his fiery, passionate nature gradually calms down into melancholy resignation.

In 1801 the object of his passion appears to have been

Giulietta Guicciardi, whom he immortalised in the dedication of the famous (so-called) "Moonlight" Sonata, Opus 27 (1802). "I now see things in a better light," he writes to Wegeler, "and associate more with my kind.... This change has been brought about by the charm of a dear girl; she loves me and I love her. These are the first happy moments I have had for two years." [1] He paid dearly for them. From the first, this love made him feel more keenly the misery of the infirmity which had overtaken him and the precarious conditions of his life which made it impossible for him to marry the one he loved. Moreover, Giulietta was a flirt, childish and selfish by nature; she made Beethoven suffer most cruelly, and in November 1803, she married Count Gallenberg. [2] Such passions devastate the soul; indeed, when the spirit is already enfeebled by illness, as was Beethoven's, complete disaster is risked. This was the only time in Beethoven's life when he seems to have been on the point of succumbing. He passed the terrible crisis, however, and the details are given in a letter known as the *Heiligenstadt Testament* to his brothers Karl and Johann, with the following direction:

---

[1] To Wegeler, 16 November, 1801.

[2] She was not afraid either of boasting of her old love for Beethoven in preference to that for her husband. Beethoven helped Gallenberg. "He was my enemy; that is the very reason why I should do all possible for him," he told Schindler on one of his conversation note-books in 1821. But he scorned to take advantage of the position. "Having arrived in Vienna," he wrote in French, "she sought me out and came weeping to me, but I rejected her."

"To be read and carried out after my death." [1] It is an outcry of revolt, full of the most poignant grief. One cannot hear it without being cut to the heart. In that dark hour he was on the verge of suicide. Only his strong moral force saved him. [2] His final hopes of recovering his health disappeared. "Even the lofty courage which has hitherto sustained me has now disappeared. O Providence, grant that but a single day of real happiness may be mine once again. I have been a stranger to the thrill of joy for so long. When, O God, when shall I feel joy once more?... Ever again? No, that would be too cruel!"

This is indeed a cry of a torn heart, and Beethoven was destined to live yet twenty-five years longer. His powerful nature would not refuse to sink beneath the weight of his woe. "My physical strength improves always with the growth of my intellectual force.... Yes, I really feel that my youth is only just beginning. Each day brings me nearer to my goal, which I can feel without being able to define clearly.... O, if I were only free from my deafness I would embrace the world!... No rest! At least, none that I know of except sleep; and I am so unhappy

---

[1] 6th October, 1802.

[2] "Bring up your children to be virtuous. That alone can make them happy; money will not. I speak from experience. It is that which sustained me in my misery. Virtue and Art alone have saved me from taking my own life." And in another letter, 2nd May, 1810, to Wegeler: "If I had not read somewhere that a man ought not to take his own life so long as he can still do a kind action, I should long ago have ended my existence, and doubtless by my own hand."

that I have to give more time to it than formerly. If only I could be free of a part of my infirmity; and then... no, I can bear it no longer. I will wage war against destiny. It shall not overcome me completely. Oh, how fine it would be to live a thousand lives in one!"[1]

This love of his, this suffering, this resignation, these alternations of dejection and pride, these "soul-tragedies" are all reflected in the great compositions written in 1802—the Sonata with the Funeral March, Opus 26; the *Sonata quasi una Fantasia*, Opus 27, No. 2; the Sonata called the "Moonlight," Opus 27; the Sonata in D Minor, Opus 31, No. 2, with its dramatic recitatives which seem like some grand yet heart-broken monologue; the Sonata in C minor for Violin, Opus 30, dedicated to the Emperor Alexander; the Kreutzer Sonata, Opus 47; and the Six Religious Songs, heroic yet grief-laden, to the words of Gellert, Opus 48. *The Second Symphony* written in 1803 reflects rather his youthful love; and here one feels that his will is decidedly gaining the upper hand. An irresistible force sweeps away his sad thoughts, a veritable bubbling over of life shows itself in the finale. Beethoven was determined to be happy. He was not willing to believe his misfortune hopeless, he wanted health, he wanted love, and he threw aside despair.[2]

---

[1] To Wegeler.

[2] Hornemann's miniature, of 1802, represents Beethoven dressed in the fashion of the day with side whiskers, long hair, the tragic air of one of Byron's heroes, but with the firm Napoleonic look which never gives way.

In many of his works one is struck by the powerful and energetic march rhythms, full of the fighting spirit. This is especially noticeable in the *Allegro* and the *Finale of Second Symphony*, and still more in the first movement, full of superb heroism, of the Violin Sonata dedicated to the Emperor Alexander. The war-like character of this music recalls the period in which it was written. The Revolution had reached Vienna. Beethoven was completely carried away by it. "He spoke freely amongst his intimate friends," said the Chevalier de Seyfried, "on political affairs, which he estimated with unusual intelligence, with a clear and well-balanced out-look. All his sympathies leaned towards revolutionary ideas." He liked the Republican principles. Schindler, the friend who knew him best during the last period of his life, said, "He was an upholder of unlimited liberty and of national independence... he desired that everyone should take part in the government of the State.... For France he desired universal suffrage and hoped that Bonaparte would establish it, thus laying down the proper basis of human happiness." A Roman of the revolutionary type, brought up on Plutarch, he dreamt of a triumphant Republic, founded by the god of victory, the first Consul. And blow by blow he forged *the Eroica Symphony*,

Bonaparte, 1804, [1] the *Iliad* of Empire, and *the Finale of the Symphony in C minor,* 1805 to 1808, the grand epic of glory. This is really the first music breathing the revolutionary feeling. The soul of the times lives again in it with the intensity and purity which great events have for those mighty and solitary souls who live apart and whose impressions are not contaminated by contact with the reality. Beethoven's spirit reveals itself, marked with stirring events, coloured by the reflections of these great wars. Evidences of this, (perhaps unconscious to him) crop up

---

[1] It is a fact that *the Eroica Symphony* was written for and around Bonaparte, and the first MS. still bears the title, "Bonaparte." Afterwards Beethoven learnt of the Coronation of Napoleon. Breaking out into a fury, he cried: "He is only an ordinary man"; and in his indignation he tore off the dedication and wrote the avenging and touching title: *Sinfonia Eroica composta per festeggiare il souvenire di un grand Uomo.* (Heroic Symphony composed to celebrate the memory of a great man). Schindler relates that later on his scorn for Napoleon became more subdued; he saw in him rather the unfortunate victim of circumstances worthy of pity, an Icarus flung down from Heaven. When he heard of the St. Helena catastrophe in 1821, he remarked: "I composed the music suitable for this sad event some seventeen years ago." It pleased him to recognise in the Funeral March of his Symphony a presentiment of the conqueror's tragic end. There was then probably in the *Eroica Symphony* and especially in the first movement, a kind of portrait of Bonaparte in Beethoven's mind, doubtless very different from the real man, and rather what he imagined him to be or would have liked him to be—the genius of the Revolution. Beethoven, in the Finale of the Eroica Symphony, used again one of the chief phrases of the work he had already written on the revolutionary hero par excellence, the god of liberty, Prometheus, 1801.

everywhere in the works of this period, in the *Coriolanus Overture* (1807), where tempests roar over the scene; in *the Fourth Quartet,* Opus 18, the first movement of which shows a close relation to this Overture; in the *Sonata Appassionata,* Op. 57 (1804), of which Bismarck said, "If I heard that often I should always be very valiant"; [1] in the score of *Egmont;* and even in his Pianoforte Concertos, in the one in E flat, Opus 73 (1809), where even the virtuosity is heroic: whole armies of warriors pass by. Nor need we be astonished at this. Though when writing the Funeral March on the death of an hero (Sonata, Opus 26), Beethoven was ignorant that the hero most worthy of his music, namely Hoche, the one who approximated more closely than Bonaparte to the model of the *Eroica Symphony,* had just died near the Rhine, where indeed his tomb stands at the top of a small hill between Coblentz and Bonn.... He had twice seen the Revolution victorious in Vienna itself. French officers were present at the first production of *Fidelio* in Vienna in November, 1805. It was General Hulin, the conqueror of the Bastille, who stayed with Lobkovitz, Beethoven's friend and protector, to whom he dedicated the Eroica and the C minor Symphony. And on 10

---

[1] Robert de Keudell, German Ambassador in Rome: *Bismarck and his family,* 1901. Robert de Keudell played this Sonata to Bismarck on an indifferent piano on 30th October, 1870, at Versailles. Bismarck remarked regarding the latter part of the work: "The sighs and struggles of a whole life are in this music." He preferred Beethoven to all other composers, and more than once affirmed "Beethoven's music more than any other soothes my nerves."

Drawing by Willibrord Joseph Mähler, 1804

May, 1809, Napoleon slept at Schönbrunn. [1]

Beethoven suddenly broke off *the C minor Symphony* to write *the Fourth Symphony* at a single sitting without his usual sketches. Happiness had come to him. In May 1806, he was betrothed to Theresa von Brunswick. [2] She had loved him for a long

---

[1]   Beethoven's house was situated near those fortifications of Vienna which Napoleon had blown up after the taking of the city. "What an awful life, with ruins all around me," wrote Beethoven to the publishers, Breitkopf & Härtel, on 26th June, 1809 "nothing but drums, trumpets, and misery of every kind." A portrait of Beethoven at this time has been left to us by a Frenchman who saw him in Vienna in 1809, Baron Trémont, of the Council of State. It gives a picturesque description of the disorder in Beethoven's room. They talked together of philosophy, religion, politics, and "especially of Shakespeare." Beethoven was very much inclined to follow Trémont to Paris, where he knew they had already performed his Symphonies at the Conservatoire, and there he had many enthusiastic admirers. (See *Mercure Musical*, 1 May, 1906, *Une visite à Beethoven*, by Baron Trémont, published by J. Chantavoine).

[2]   Or to be more exact, Theresa Brunsvik. Beethoven had met the Brunsviks at Vienna between 1796 and 1799. Giulietta Guicciardi was the cousin of Theresa. Beethoven seems also to have been attracted at one period by one of Theresa's sisters, Josephine, who first married Count Deym, and later on, the Baron Stackelberg. Some very striking details on the Brunsvik family are found in an article by M. André de Hevesy. *Beethoven et l'Immortelle Bien-aimée* (*Revue de Paris*, March 1 and 15, 1910). For this study M. de Hevesy has made use of the MS. Memoires and the papers of Theresa, which were preserved at Martonvasar in Hungary. They all show an affectionate intimacy between Beethoven and the Brunsviks, and raise again the question of his love for Theresa. But the arguments are not convincing, and I leave them to be discussed at some future time.

time—ever since as a young girl she had taken piano lessons from him during his first stay in Vienna. Beethoven was a friend of her brother Count Franz. In 1806 he stayed with them at Martonvasar in Hungary, and it was there that they fell in love. The remembrance of these happy days is kept fresh by some stories in some of Theresa's writings. [1] "One Sunday evening," she says, "after dinner, with the moon shining into the room, Beethoven was seated at the piano. At first he laid his hands flat on the keyboard. Franz and I always understood this, for it was his usual preparation. Then he struck some chords in the bass and slowly with an air of solemnity and mystery drifted into a song of John Sebastian Bach: '*If thou wilt give me thy heart, first let it be in secret, that our hearts may commingle and no one divine it.*' [2]

"My mother and the priest had fallen asleep and my brother was dream gazing whilst I who understood his song and his expression, felt life come to me in all its fullness. The following morning we met in the park and he said to me, 'I am now writing an opera; the principal character is in me and around me wherever I go. Never before have I reached such heights of happiness; I feel light, purity and splendour all around me and within. Until now I have been like the child in

---

[1] Marian Tanger: *Beethovens unsterbliche Geliebte* (Beethoven's undying Love), Bonn, 1890.

[2] *Wilst du dein Herz mir schenken (Aria di Govannini)*, Edition Peters, 2071. This beautiful air appears in the album which Bach wrote for his wife, Anna Magdalena.

the fairy story, picking up pebbles along the road without seeing the beautiful flower blossoming close by.'... It was in May, 1806, that I became betrothed to him with the ready consent of my dear brother Franz."

The *Fourth Symphony* composed in this year is a pure fragrant flower which treasures up the perfume of these days, the calmest in all his life. It has been justly remarked that at this time "Beethoven's desire was to reconcile his genius as far as possible with what was generally known and admired in the forms handed down by his predecessors." [1] The same conciliating spirit springing from this love re-acted on his manners and his way of living in general. Ignaz von Seyfried and Grillparzer say that he was full of life, bright, happy and witty, courteous in society, patient with tedious people and careful in his dress. Even his deafness was not noticed, and they say that he was in good health with the exception of his eyesight, which was rather weak. [2] This strikes one in looking at Mahler's portrait of him painted at this time, in which he is represented with an elegance unusual for him and a romantic,

---

[1] Nohl: *Life of Beethoven.*

[2] Beethoven was really short-sighted. Ignaz von Seyfried says that this was caused by smallpox, and that he was obliged to wear spectacles when quite young. This short-sightedness would probably exaggerate the wild expression of his eyes. His letters between 1823-1824 contain frequent complaints on the subject of his eyes which were often painful. See the articles by Christian Kalischer on this subject, *Beethovens Augens und Augenleiden* (*Die Musik*, 15th March—1st April, 1902).

even slightly affected look. Beethoven wishes to please, and rather fancies himself in doing so. The lion is in love; he draws in his claws. But one feels deep beneath under all this playfulness, the imagination and tenderness of *the Symphony in B flat*, the tremendous force, the capricious humour and the passionate temper of his nature.

This profound peace was not destined to last although love exercised its soothing influence until 1810. Beethoven doubtless owed to it the self-mastery which at this period enabled him to produce some of the most perfect fruits of his genius; that great classical tragedy, the Symphony in C minor and that delicious idyll of a summer's day: *the Pastoral Symphony*, 1808. [1] *The Sonata Appassionata*, inspired by Shakespeare's *Tempest*,[2] the Sonata which he himself regarded as his most powerful one, appeared in 1807 and was dedicated to Theresa's brother. To Theresa herself he dedicated the dreamy and fantastic Sonata in F sharp, Opus 78 (1809). An undated letter addressed to his "Immortal Beloved" expresses the intensity of his love no less strongly than does the *Sonata Appassionata*.

July (1801).

---

[1]   The music for Goethe's play *Egmont* was commenced in 1809. Beethoven had also wished to write the music to *William Tell*, but Gyrovetz was chosen before him.

[2]   Conversation with Schindler.

My Angel, my all, my very self.

Just a few words to-day—and indeed in pencil (with thine). Only till to-morrow is my room definitely engaged. What an unworthy waste of time in such matters! Why this deep sorrow where necessity speaks? Can our love endure otherwise than through sacrifices, through restraint in longing? Canst thou help not being wholly mine? Can I, not being wholly thine? Oh! gaze at nature in all its beauty, and calmly accept the inevitable—love demands everything, and rightly so. Thus is it for me with thee, for thee with me, only thou so easily forgettest that I must live for myself and for thee. Were we wholly united, thou wouldst feel this painful fact as little as I should. My journey was terrible. I arrived here only yesterday morning at four o'clock, and as they were short of horses, the mail-coach selected another route; but what an awful road! At the last stage but one, I was advised not to travel by night; they warned me against the wood, but that only spurred me on, and I was wrong; the coach must needs break down, the road being dreadful, a swamp, a mere country road; without the postillions I had with me I should have stuck on the way. Esterhazy, by the ordinary road, met the same fate with eight horses as I with four—yet it gave me some pleasure, as successfully overcoming any difficulty always does. Now for a quick change from without to within; we shall probably soon see each other; besides, to-day I cannot tell thee what has been passing through my mind

during the past few days concerning my life. Were our hearts
closely united I should not do things of this kind. My heart
is full of the many things I have to say to thee. Ah! there are
moments in which I feel that speech is powerless. Cheer up.
Remain my true, my only treasure, my all!!! As I to thee. The
gods must send the rest; what is in store for us must be and
ought to be.

> *Thy faithful*
> *LUDWIG.*

It is difficult to divine what was the barrier which separated these two from the consummation of their love. Was it the lack of fortune or the difference in social position? Perhaps Beethoven rebelled against the long period of probation which was imposed on him or resented the humiliation of keeping his love secret for an indefinite period.

Perhaps, impulsive and afflicted as he was, a misanthrope too, he caused his loved one to suffer without wishing it and gave himself up to despair in consequence. The fact remains that the engagement was broken off, although neither seems ever to have proved faithless. Even to her last day (she lived till 1861) Theresa von Brunswick loved Beethoven, and Beethoven was no less faithful.

In 1816 he remarked, "When I think of her my heart beats as violently as on the day when I first saw her." To this year belong the six songs, Opus 98, which have so touching and profound a feeling. They are dedicated "To the loved one far away" (*An die ferne Geliebte*). He wrote in his notes, "My heart overflows at the thought of her beautiful nature; and yet she is not here, not near me!" Theresa had given her portrait to Beethoven, inscribed, "To the rare genius, the great artist, the generous man. T.B." [1] Once during the last year of his life a friend surprised Beethoven alone, and found him holding this portrait and speaking to himself through his tears: "Thou wert so lovely and great, so like to an angel!" The friend withdrew, and returning a little later found him at the piano, and said "To-day, my old friend, there are no black looks on your face." Beethoven replied "It is because my good angel has visited me." The wound was deep. "Poor Beethoven," he said to himself, "there is no happiness for you in this world; only in the realms of the ideal will you find strength to conquer yourself." [2]

In his notebook he wrote, "submission, complete submission to your destiny. You can no longer live for yourself, only for others. For you there is happiness only in your art. O God, give me strength to conquer "myself.""...

Love then abandoned him. In 1810 he was once more alone; but joy had come to him and the consciousness of his

---

[1]   This portrait can still be seen in Beethoven's house at Bonn. It is reproduced in Frimmel's *Life of Beethoven*, page 29, and in the "Musical Times," 15th December, 1892.

[2]   To Gleichen stein.

power. He was in the prime of life. He gave himself up to his violent and wild moods regardless of results, and certainly without care for the opinions of the world and the usual conventions of life. What, indeed, had he to fear or to be careful of? Gone are love and ambition. Strength and the joy of it, the necessity for using it, almost abusing it, were left to him. "Power constitutes the morality of men who distinguish themselves above the ordinary." He returned to his neglect in matters of dress, and his manners now became even freer than before. He knew that he had the right to speak freely even to the greatest. "I recognise no sign of superiority in mankind other than goodness," he writes on 17 July, 1812. [1] Bettina Brentano, who saw him at that time, says that "no king or emperor was ever so conscious of his power." She was fascinated by his very strength. "When I saw him for the first time," she wrote to Goethe, "the whole exterior world vanished from me. Beethoven made me forget the world, and even you, O Goethe.... I do not think I am wrong in saying this man is very far ahead of modern civilisation."

---

[1] "The heart is the mainspring of all that is great" (to Giannatasio del Rio).

Goethe attempted to make Beethoven's acquaintance. [1]
They met at a Bohemian spa, Töplitz, in 1812, but did not agree
well. Beethoven passionately admired Goethe's genius; but
his own character was too free and too wild not to wound the
susceptibilities of Goethe. Beethoven himself has told us of
this walk which they took together, in the course of which the
haughty republican gave the courtly councillor of the Grand-
duke of Weimar a lesson in dignity which he never forgot.

*"Kings and princes can easily make professors and
privy councillors; they can bestow titles and decorations, but
they cannot make great men, or minds which rise above the*

---

[1] "Goethe's poems give me great happiness," he wrote to Bettina
Brentano on 19th February, 1811. And also "Goethe and Schiller are my
favourite poets, together with Ossian and Homer, whom, unfortunately, I
can only read in translations." To Breitkopf & Härtel, 8th August, 1809,
Nohl, *New Letters*, LIII.

It is remarkable that Beethoven's taste in literature was so sound in
view of his neglected education. In addition to Goethe, who he said
was "grand, majestic, always in D major" (and more than Goethe)
he loved three men, Homer, Plutarch and Shakespeare. Of Homer's
works he preferred the *Odyssey* to the *Iliad*; he was continually reading
Shakespeare (from a German translation) and we know with what tragic
grandeur he has set *Coriolanus* and the *Tempest* in music. He read
Plutarch continually, as did all who were in favour of the revolution.
Brutus was his hero, as was also the case with Michael Angelo; he had
a small statue of him in his bedroom. He loved Plato, and dreamed of
establishing his republic in the whole world. "Socrates and Jesus have
been my models," he wrote once on his notebooks (Conversations
during 1819 and 1820).

base turmoil of this world ... and when two men are together such as Goethe and myself these fine gentlemen must be made conscious of the difference between ourselves and them. Yesterday, as we were returning home on foot, we met the whole of the Imperial family. We saw them approaching from a distance. Goethe let go my arm to take his stand by the road side with the crowd. It was in vain that I talked to him. Say what I would I could not get him to move a single step. I drew my hat down upon my head, buttoned up my overcoat, and forced my way through the throng. Princes and courtiers stood aside. Duke Rudolph raised his hat to me, the Empress bowing to me first. The great of the earth know me and recognise me. I amused myself in watching the procession pass by Goethe. He remained on the road side bowing low, hat in hand. I took him to task for it pretty severely and did not spare him at all." [1]

Nor did Goethe forget the scene. [2]

---

[1] To Bettina von Arnim. The authenticity of Beethoven's letters to Bettina, doubted by Schindler, Marx and Deiters, has been supported by Moritz Carriere, Nohl and Kalischer. Bettina has perhaps embellished them a little, but the foundation remains reliable.

[2] "Beethoven," said Goethe to Zelter, "is, unfortunately, possessed of a wild and uncouth disposition; doubtless, he is not wrong in finding the world detestable, but that is not the way to make it pleasant for himself or for others. We must excuse and pity him for he is deaf." After that he did nothing against Beethoven nor did he do anything for him, but he ignored him completely. At the bottom, however, he admired Beethoven's

In 1812 *the Seventh* and *Eighth Symphonies* were written during a stay of several months at Töplitz. These works are veritable orgies of rhythm and humour; in them he is perhaps revealing himself in his most natural and as he styled it himself, most "unbuttoned" (*aufgeknöpft*) moods, transports of gaiety contrasting unexpectedly with storms of fury and disconcerting flashes of wit followed by those Titanic explosions which terrified both Goethe and Zelter [1] and caused the remark in North Germany that the *Symphony in A* was the work of a drunkard. The work of an inebriated man indeed it was, but one intoxicated with power

---

music and feared it also. He was afraid it would cause him to lose that mental calm which he had gained through so much trouble. A letter of young Felix Mendelssohn, who passed through Weimar in 1830, gives us a very interesting glimpse into the depths of that storm-tossed passionate soul controlled as it was by a masterly and powerful intellect.... "At first," writes Mendelssohn, "he did not want to hear Beethoven's name mentioned, but after a time he was persuaded to listen to *the First Movement of the Symphony in C minor*, which moved him deeply. He would not show anything outwardly, but merely remarked to me, 'that does not touch me, it only surprises me.' After a time he said 'It is really grand, it is maddening, you would think the house was crumbling to pieces.' Afterwards, at dinner, he sat pensive and absorbed until he began to question me about Beethoven's music. I saw quite clearly that a deep impression had been made on him...." (For information on the relations between Goethe and Beethoven, see various articles by Frimmel).

[1] Letter from Goethe to Zelter, 2nd September, 1812.... Zelter to Goethe, 14th September, 1812: "*Auch ich bewundere ihn mit Schrecken*" ("I, too, regard him with mingled admiration and dread"). Zelter writes to Goethe in 1819, "They say he is mad."

and genius; one who said of himself, "I am the Bacchus who crushes delicious nectar for mankind. It is I who give the divine frenzy to men."

Wagner wrote, "I do not know whether Beethoven wished to depict a Dionysian orgy [1] in the *Finale of his Symphony*, though I recognise in this passionate *kermesse* a sign of his Flemish origin, just as we see it likewise in his bold manner of speech and in his bearing so free and so utterly out of harmony with a country ruled by an iron discipline and rigid etiquette. Nowhere is there greater frankness or freer power than in the *Symphony in A*. It is a mad outburst of superhuman energy, with no other object than for the pleasure of unloosing it like a river overflowing its banks and flooding the surrounding country. In *the Eighth Symphony* the power is not so sublime, though it is still more strange and characteristic of the man, mingling tragedy with farce and a Herculean vigour with the games and caprices of a child." [2]

The year 1814 marks the summit of Beethoven's fortunes. At the Vienna Congress he enjoyed European fame. He took an active part in the fêtes, princes rendered him homage, and (as he afterwards boasted to Schindler) he allowed himself to be

---

[1] At any rate, this was a subject which Beethoven had in his mind; for we find it in his notes, especially those for the proposed Tenth Symphony.

[2] There was a very tender intimacy between Amalie Sebald and him about this time, and it is possible that this may have supplied the inspiration.

courted by them.

He was carried away by his sympathy with the War of Independence. [1] In 1813 he wrote a Symphony on *Wellington's Victory* and in the beginning of 1814 a martial chorus, *Germany's Rebirth* (*Germanias Wiedergeburt*). On November 29th, 1814, he conducted before an audience of kings a patriotic Cantata, *The Glorious Moment* (*Der glorreiche Augenblick*), and on the occasion of the capture of Paris in 1815 he composed a Chorus, *It is accomplished* (*Es ist vollbracht*). These occasional pieces did more to spread his fame than all the rest of his music together. The engraving by Blasius Hoefel from a sketch by the Frenchman Latronne and the savage-looking cast by Franz Klein in 1812 present a lifelike image of Beethoven at the time of the Congress of Vienna. The dominating characteristic of this leonine face with its firm set jaws scored with the furrows of anger and trouble, is determination—a Napoleonic will. One recognises the man who said of Napoleon after Jena, "How unfortunate that I do not know as much about warfare as music! I would show myself his master."

But his kingdom was not of this world. "My empire is in the air," he wrote to Franz von Brunswick. [2]

---

[1] Differing from him in this, Schubert had written in 1807 a *pièce d'occasion*, in honour of Napoleon the Great, and conducted the performance himself before the Emperor.

[2] "I say nothing of our monarchs and their kingdoms," he wrote to Kauka during the Congress. "To my mind, the empire of the spirit is the dearest of all. It is the first of all kingdoms, temporal and spiritual."

After this hour of glory comes the saddest and most miserable period.

Vienna had never been sympathetic to Beethoven. Haughty and bold genius as he was, he could not be at ease in this frivolous city with its mundane and its mediocre spirit, which Wagner laughed to scorn later on. [1] He lost no opportunities of going away; and towards 1808 he thought seriously of leaving Austria to go to the court of Jerome Bonaparte, King of Westphalia. [2] But Vienna had abundant musical resources; and one must do it justice by saying that there were always noble *dilettanti* who felt the grandeur of Beethoven, and who

---

[1] Vienna, is that not to say everything? All trace of German Protestantism eradicated, even the national accent lost, Italianised.... German spirit, German habits and ways explained from textbooks of Italian and Spanish origin.... The country of debased history, falsified science, falsified religion.... A frivolous scepticism calculated to undermine all love of truth, honour, and independence! (Wagner, *Beethoven*, 1870).

Grillparzer has written that it was a misfortune to be born an Austrian. The great German composers of the end of the 19th Century who have lived in Vienna, have suffered cruelly from the spirit of this town, delivered up to the Pharisaical cult of Brahms. The life of Bruckner was one long martyrdom. Hugo Wolf, who battled furiously before giving in, has uttered implacable judgments on Vienna.

[2] King Jerome had offered Beethoven an annuity of six hundred ducats of gold and 150 silver ducats for travelling expenses, for playing to him occasionally and for managing his chamber-music concerts, which were not long or very frequent. Beethoven was eager to go.

spared their country the shame of losing him. In 1809, three of the richest noblemen of Vienna, the Archduke Rudolph, a pupil of Beethoven, Prince Lobkovitz and Prince Kinsky undertook to pay him annually a pension of 4,000 florins on the sole condition that he remained in Austria. "As it is evident," they said, "that a man can only devote himself entirely to art when he is free from all material care, and that it is only then that he can produce such sublime works which are the glory of art, the undersigned have formed a resolution to release Ludwig van Beethoven from the shadow of need, and thus disperse the miserable obstacles which are so detrimental to his flights of genius."

Unhappily the results did not come up to the promises. The pension was always very irregularly paid; soon it ceased altogether. Also Vienna had very much changed in character after the Congress of 1814. Society was distracted from art by politics. Musical taste was spoilt by Italianism, and the fashionable people favoured Rossini, treating Beethoven as pedantic. [1] Beethoven's friends and protectors went away or

---

[1] Rossini's *Tancredi* sufficed to shake the whole German musical edifice. Bauernfold (quoted by Ehrhard) notes in his *Journal* this criticism which circulated in the Viennese salons in 1816: "Mozart and Beethoven are old pedants; the stupidity of the preceding period amused them: it is only since Rossini that one has really known melody. *Fidelio* is quite devoid of music; one cannot understand why people take the trouble to weary themselves with it." Beethoven gave his last concert as pianist in 1814.

died: Prince Kinsky in 1812, Lichnovsky in 1814, Lobkovitz in 1816. Rasumowsky, for whom he had written the three admirable Quartets, Opus 59, gave his last concert in February, 1815. In 1815 Beethoven quarrelled with Stephen von Breuning, the friend of his childhood, the brother of Eleonore. [1] From this time he was alone. [2] "I have no friends. I am alone in the world" he wrote in his notebook of 1816.

His deafness became complete. [3] After the autumn of 1815 he could only communicate with his friends by writing. [4] The oldest conversation book is dated 1816. [5] There is a sad story recorded by Schindler with regard to the representation of *Fidelio* in 1822.

"Beethoven wanted to conduct the general rehearsal....

---

[1]　The same year Beethoven lost his brother Karl. "He clung to life so, that I would willingly have given mine," he wrote to Antonia Brentano.

[2]　Except for his intimate friendship with Countess Maria von Erdödy, a constant sufferer like himself, afflicted with an incurable malady. She lost her only son suddenly in 1816. Beethoven dedicated to her in 1809 his two Trios Op. 70; and in 1815-17, his two great Sonatas for Violoncello Op. 102.

[3]　Besides his deafness, his health grew worse from day to day. During October, 1816, he was very ill. In the summer of 1817 his doctor said he had a chest complaint. During the winter, 1817-18, he was tormented with his so-called phthisis. Then he had acute rheumatism in 1820-21, jaundice in 1821, and several maladies in 1823.

[4]　A change of style in his music, beginning with the Sonata Op: 101, dates from this time.

[5]　Beethoven's conversation-books form more than 11,000 manuscript pages, and can be found bound to-day in the Imperial Library at Berlin.

From the duet of the First Act, it was evident that he could hear nothing of what was going on. He kept back the pace considerably; and whilst the orchestra followed his beat, the singer hurried the time. There followed general confusion. The usual leader of the orchestra, Umlauf, suggested a short rest, without giving any reason; and after exchanging a few words with the singers, they began again. The same disorder broke out afresh. Another interval was necessary. The impossibility of continuing under Beethoven's direction was evident; but how could they make him understand? No one had the heart to say to him, 'Go away, poor unfortunate one, you cannot conduct.' Beethoven, uneasy and agitated, turned from side to side, trying to read the expression of the different faces, and to understand what the difficulty was: a silence came over all. Suddenly he called me in his imperious manner. When I was quite near to him, he handed me his pocket-book, and made signs to me to write. I put down these words: 'I beg you not to continue; I will explain why at your house.' With one leap he jumped from the platform, saying to me, 'Let us go quickly.' He ran straight to his house, went in and threw himself down on a sofa, covering his face with his hands; he remained like that until dinner-time. At the table it was impossible to draw a word from him; he wore an expression of complete despondency and profound grief. After dinner when I wanted to leave him, he kept me, expressing a desire not to be left alone. When we separated he asked me to go with him to his doctor, who had a great reputation for

Drawing by Joseph Willibrord Mähler, 1815

complaints of the ear. During the whole of my connection with Beethoven I do not know of any day which can compare with this awful day of November. He had been smitten to the heart, and until the day of his death, he retained the impression of this terrible scene."[1]

Two years later, on 7 May, 1824, when conducting the *Choral Symphony* (or rather, as the programme said, "taking part in the direction of the concert") he heard nothing at all of the clamour of the audience applauding him. He did not even suspect it, until one of the singers, taking him by the hand turned him round; and he suddenly saw the audience waving their hats and clapping their hands. An English traveller, Russell, who saw him at the piano about the year 1825, says that when he wanted to play quietly the notes did not sound and that it was very moving to follow in silence the emotion animating him expressed in his face, and in the movements of his fingers.

Buried in himself,[2] and separated from all mankind, his only consolation was in Nature. "She was his sole confident," says Theresa of Brunswick, "she was his refuge." Charles Neate, who knew him in 1815, says that he never saw anyone who loved flowers, clouds and nature so devotedly; he seemed

---

[1] Schindler, who had been intimate with Beethoven since 1819, had known him slightly since 1814; but Beethoven had found it very difficult to be friendly; he treated him at first with disdainful haughtiness.

[2] See the admirable notes of Wagner on Beethoven's deafness (*Beethoven*, 1870).

to live in them. [1] "No one on earth can love the country so much as I," wrote Beethoven. "I love a tree more than a man." When in Vienna he walked round the ramparts every day. In the country from daybreak till night he walked alone, without hat, in sunshine or rain. "Almighty God! In the woods I am happy, happy in the woods, where each tree speaks through Thee. O God, what splendour! In the forests, on the hills, it is the calm, the quiet, that helps me."

His unrestfulness of mind found some respite there. [2] He was harassed by financial cares. He wrote in 1818, "I am almost reduced to beggary, and I am obliged to pretend that I do not lack necessities"; and at another time, "The *Sonata Op. 106* has been written under pressing circumstances. It is a hard thing to have to work for bread." Spohr says that often he could not go out on account of his worn-out shoes. He owed large debts to his publishers and his compositions did not bring him in anything. The *Mass in D*, published by subscription, obtained only seven subscribers (of whom not one was a musician). [3] He

---

[1] He loved animals and pitied them. The mother of the historian, von Frimmel, says that for a long while she had an involuntary dislike for Beethoven, because when she was a little girl he drove away with his handkerchief all the butterflies that she wanted to catch.

[2] He was always uncomfortable in his lodgings. In thirty-five years in Vienna, he changed his rooms thirty times.

[3] Beethoven had written personally to Cherubini, who was "of all his contemporaries the one whom he most esteemed." Cherubini did not reply.

received barely thirty or forty ducats for his fine Sonatas, each one of which cost him three months' work. The Quartets, *Opp.* 127, 130, and 132, amongst his profoundest works, which seem to be written with his very heart-blood, were written for Prince Galitzin, who neglected to pay for them. Beethoven was worn out with domestic difficulties, and with endless law suits to obtain the pensions owing to him or to retain the guardianship of a nephew, the son of his brother Karl, who died of consumption in 1815.

He had bestowed on this child all the care and devotion with which his heart overflowed. But he was repaid with cruel suffering. It seemed that a kind of special fate had taken care to renew ceaselessly and to accumulate his miseries in order that his genius should not lack for food. At first he had a dispute over Karl with his mother, who wanted to take him away.

"O, my God," he cried, "my shield and my defence, my only refuge! Thou readest the depths of my soul and Thou knowest the griefs that I experience when I have to cause suffering to those who want to dispute my Karl, my treasure.[1] Hearken unto me, Great Being, that I know not how to name. Grant the fervent prayer of the most unhappy of Thy creatures!"

"O God, aid me! Thou wilt not leave me entirely in the

---

[1] "I never avenge myself," he wrote besides to Madame Streicher. "When I am obliged to act against others, I only do what is necessary to defend myself or to prevent them from doing one harm."

hands of men; because I do not wish to make a covenant with injustice! Hear the prayer which I make to Thee, that at least for the future I may live with my Karl!... O cruel fate, implacable destiny! No, no, my unhappiness will never end!"

Then this nephew, so passionately loved, proved unworthy of the confidence of his uncle. The correspondence between Beethoven and him is sad and revolting, like that of Michael Angelo with his brothers, but more simple and touching.

> *"Am I to be repaid once again with the most abominable ingratitude? Ah, well, if the bond must be broken, so be it! All impartial people who hear of it will hate you. If the compact between us weighs too heavily, in the name of God, may it be according to His will! I abandon you to Providence; I have done all that I could; I am ready to appear before the Supreme Judge!*
>
> *"Spoilt as you are, that should not make it difficult to teach you to be simple and true; my heart has suffered so much by your hypocritical conduct, and it is difficult for me to forget.... God is my witness, I only long to be a thousand miles from you and from that sorry brother and from this abominable family.... I shall never more have confidence in you."* And he signed *"Unhappily your father—or rather, not your father."*

But pardon came almost immediately.

"My dear son! No more of this! Come to my arms. You shall not hear one harsh word. I will receive you with the same love. We will talk over what is to be done for your future in a friendly manner. On my word of honour there will be no reproach. That would do no good. You have nothing to expect from me but sympathy and the most loving care. Come, come to the faithful heart of your father. Come immediately you receive this letter, come to the house." (And on the envelope in French, *"If you do not come, you will surely kill me."*)

"Do not deceive me," he begged, *"be always my beloved son. What a horrible discord it would be if you were to be false to me, as many persons maintain that you already are.... Good-bye, he who has not given you life but who has certainly preserved it, and who has taken all possible care with your moral development, with an affection more than paternal, begs you from the bottom of his heart to follow the only true path of the good and the just.*

Your faithful foster-father." [1]

After having cherished all kinds of dreams for the future of this nephew, who was not lacking in intelligence and whom he

---

[1]   A letter which has been found in Berlin to M. Kalischer, shews with what deep feeling Beethoven wished to make his nephew "a citizen useful to the state" (February 1st, 1819).

wished to take up a University career, Beethoven had to consent to make a merchant of him. But Karl frequented gambling dens and contracted debts.

By a sad phenomenon, more frequent than one believes, the moral grandeur of his uncle, instead of doing him good, made him worse. It exasperated him, impelling him to revolt, as he said in those terrible words where his miserable soul appears so plainly, "I have become worse because my uncle wished me to do better." He reached such a state that in the summer of 1826 he shot himself in the head with a pistol. He did not die from it, but it was Beethoven who just missed dying. He never recovered from this terrible fright. [1] Karl recovered; he lived to the end to cause suffering to his uncle, whose death he hastened in no slight measure. Nor was he with him at the hour of his death. "God has never abandoned me," wrote Beethoven to his nephew, some years before. "He will find someone to close my eyes." This was not to be the one whom he called "his son." [2]

It was from the depth of this abyss that Beethoven undertook to chant his immortal *Ode to Joy*.

It was the plan of his whole life. As early as 1793, he had

---

[1]   Schindler, who saw him then, says that he suddenly became an old man of seventy, utterly crushed and broken of will. He would have died had Karl died. He died soon afterwards.

[2]   The dilettantism of our time has not failed to seek to reinstate this scoundrel. This is not surprising.

thought of it at Bonn.[1] All his life he wished to celebrate Joy; and to make it the climax of one of his great works. He was always striving to find the exact form of the Hymn, and the work where he could place it. He was far from being decided, even in his *Ninth Symphony*. Until the very last moment, he was on the point of putting off the *Ode to Joy* to a *Tenth* or *Eleventh Symphony*. One ought to notice that the *Ninth Symphony* is not entitled *Choral Symphony*, as it is now invariably called, but *Symphony with a Final Chorus on the Ode to Joy*. It narrowly missed having another conclusion. In July, 1823, Beethoven still thought of giving it an instrumental *finale*, which he used later on for the quartet Op: 132. Both Czerny and Sonnleithner say that even after the performance in May, 1824, Beethoven had not abandoned this idea.

---

[1] Letter from Fischenich to Charlotte Schiller (January, 1793). Schiller's *Ode* was written in 1785. The actual theme appeared in 1808 in the *Fantasy for piano, orchestra and Choir, Op. 80*, and in 1810 in the Song on Goethe's words: *Kleine Blumen, Kleine Blaetter*. I have seen in a note book of 1812 belonging to Dr. Erich Prieger at Bonn, between the sketches of the *Seventh Symphony* and a plan for an *Overture to Macbeth*, an attempt to adopt some words of Schiller to the theme which he used later on in the *Overture Op. 115 (Namensfeier)*. Several instrumental motives of the *Ninth Symphony* appeared before 1815. Thus the definite theme of Joy was put down in notes in 1822; also all the other airs of the *Symphony*, except the Trio, which came a little after, then the *andante moderato*, and later the *adagio*, which appeared last of all. For references to Schiller's poem and the false interpretation which is given nowadays by substituting for the word *Joy* the word *Liberty*, see an article by Charles Andler in *Pages Libres* (July 8, 1905).

He found great technical difficulties in introducing the Chorus into the Symphony, as is shown by Beethoven's note-books and his numerous attempts to make the voices enter at another part of the work and in a different manner. In the sketches for the second subject of the Adagio [1] he wrote "Perhaps the Chorus could enter conveniently here." But he could not decide to part from his faithful orchestra. "When an idea comes to me," he said, "I hear it on an instrument, never on a voice." So he put back the place for employing voices as late as possible. At first he wanted to give the instruments not only the *recitatives of the Finale* [2] but even the Theme of Joy itself.

But we must go still further into the reason of these hesitations and delays. The explanation is very deep. Continually tormented by grief, this unfortunate man had always aspired to sing the excellence of Joy; and from year to year he put off his task, held back ceaselessly by the whirlwind of his passion and grief. It was only at the very last that he succeeded. But with what a success!

At the moment when the Theme of Joy appears for the first time, the orchestra stops abruptly, thus giving a sudden unexpected character to the entrance of the Song. And this is a true touch; this theme is rightly divine. Joy descends

---

[1]   Berlin Library.

[2]   Exactly as if it had words beneath.

from heaven enveloped in a supernatural calm; it soothes the suffering with its cool breath; and the first impression that it makes, is so tender as it steals into the sorrowing heart, that a friend of Beethoven has said "One feels inclined to weep, as one looks into those soft, calm eyes of his." When the Theme passes first to the voices, it is the Basses who present it first with a solemn and rather weighty character. But, little by little Joy takes possession of us. It is a real battle, a fight with sorrow. We can hear the rhythms of marching armies. In the ardent panting song of the tenor, in all these quivering pages we can almost feel the breath of Beethoven himself, the rhythm of his breathing and his inspired cries as he wandered across the fields, composing the work, transported by a demoniacal fury like King Lear in the middle of a storm. After the warlike joy comes religious Ecstasy. Then follows a sacred orgy, a very delirium of love. A whole trembling humanity lifts its arms to the sky, utters powerful outcries, rushes forth towards this Joy and clasps it to the heart.

This Titanic work overcame the indifference of the public. The frivolous crowds of Vienna were moved for an instant, but they still favoured Rossini and his Italian operas. Humiliated and saddened, Beethoven was on the point of going to live in London and thought of giving his *Ninth Symphony* there. A second time, as in 1809, some noble friends sent him a petition asking that he would not leave the country. They said "We know that you have written a new composition of sacred

Drawing by Joseph Karl Stieler, 1820

music [1] in which you have expressed sentiments inspired by your profound faith. The supernatural light which penetrates your great soul illumines the work. We know besides that the garland of your inspired symphonies has been increased by an immortal flower.... Your absence during these last years has troubled all those whose eyes are turned to you. [2] Everyone sadly thought that the man of genius placed so high amongst living beings remained silent whilst another kind of foreign art sought to plant itself in our country, causing the productions of German art to be forgotten.... From you only, the nation awaits new life, new laurels, and a new reign of truth and beauty, despite the fashion of the day.... Give us the hope of soon seeing our desires satisfied. And then the springtime which is coming will blossom again doubly, thanks to your gifts to us and to the world!" [3] This noble address shews what power, not only artistic but also moral, Beethoven exercised over the *élite* of Germany. The first word which occurs to his followers who

---

[1] The *Mass in D*, Op: 123.

[2] Harassed by domestic quarrels, misery, cares of all kinds, Beethoven only wrote during the five years from 1816 to 1821, three pieces for the piano (Op: 101, 102, and 106). His enemies said he was exhausted. He began to work again in 1821.

[3] February, 1824. Signed Prince C. Lichnowski, Count Maurice Lich-nowsky, Count Maurice de Fries, Count M. de Dietrichstein, Count F. de Palfy, Count Czernin, Ignace Edler de Mosel, Charles Czerny, Abbé Stadler, A. Diabelli, Artari & Co., Steiner & Co., A. Streicher, Zmeskall, Kiesewetter, etc.

wish to praise his genius is neither science, nor art; it is *faith*.[1]

Beethoven was deeply moved by these words. He stayed. On May 7th, 1824, the first performance in Vienna of the *Mass in D* and the *Ninth Symphony* took place. The success was amazing; and his greeting almost of a seditious character for when Beethoven appeared he was accorded five rounds of applause; whereas according to the strict etiquette of the city, it was the custom to give three only for the entrance of the Royal Family. The police had to put an end to the manifestations. The Symphony raised frantic enthusiasm. Many wept. Beethoven fainted with emotion after the concert; he was taken to Schindler's house where he remained asleep all the night and the following morning, fully dressed, neither eating nor drinking. The triumph was only fleeting, however, and the concert brought in nothing for Beethoven. His material circumstances of life were not changed

---

[1] "My moral character is publicly recognised," Beethoven proudly said to the Vienna Municipality, on February 1st, 1819, to vindicate his right to the guardianship of his nephew. Even distinguished writers like Weisenbach have considered him worthy of the dedication of their works.

by it. He found himself poor, ill, [1] alone but a conqueror: [2] conqueror of the mediocrity of mankind, conqueror of his destiny, conqueror of his suffering.

"Sacrifice, always sacrifice the trifles of life to art! God is over all!"

He had then completed the object of his whole life. He had tasted perfect Joy. Would he be able to rest on this triumph of the soul which ruled the tempest? Certainly he ought to feel the relief from the days of his past anguish. Indeed his last quartets are full of strange forebodings. But it seems that the victory of the *Ninth Symphony* had left its glorious traces in its nature. The plans which he had for the future: [3] the *Tenth*

---

[1]   In August, 1824, he was haunted with the fear of sudden death "like my grandfather to whom I bear so much resemblance," he wrote on August 16th, 1824, to Dr. Bach.

[2]   *The Ninth Symphony* was given for the first time in Germany at Frankfurt on April 1st, 1825; in London on March 25th, 1825; in Paris at the Conservatoire on March 27th, 1831. Mendelssohn, then aged seventeen, gave a performance of it on the piano at the Jaegerhalle in Berlin on November 14th, 1826. Wagner, a student at Leipzig, re-copied it entirelyby hand; and in a letter, dated October 6th, 1830, to the publisher, Schott, offered him a reduction of the Symphony for pianoforte duet. One can say that the Ninth Symphony decided Wagner's career.

[3]   "Apollo and his Muses would not wish to deliver me up to death yet, for I still owe them so much. Before I go to the Champs-Elysée I must leave behind me what the spirit inspires and tells me to finish. It seems to me that I have scarcely written anything." (To the brothers Schott, Sept. 17th, 1824.)

Symphony, [1] the overture on the name of BACH, the music for Grillparzer's *Melusina*, [2] for Körner's *Odyssey* and Goethe's *Faust*, [3] the Biblical oratorio of *Saul and David*, all shew that he was attracted by the mighty serenity of the old German masters—Bach and Handel—and more still to the light of the South—the South of France or Italy, where he hoped to

---

[1]   Beethoven wrote to Moscheles on March 18th, 1827: "The complete sketch of a Symphony is in my desk with a new overture." This sketch has never been found. One only reads in his notes:
"Adagio cantique." Religious song for a symphony in the old modes (*Herr Gott dich loben wir.—Alleluja*), may be in an independent style, may be as introduction to a fugue. This Symphony might be characterised by the entrance of voices, perhaps in the *finale*, perhaps in the *adagio*. The violins in the orchestra, etc., increased ten times for the last movements. The voices to enter one by one; or to repeat the *adagio* somehow in the last movements. For words for the *adagio*, a Greek myth or an ecclesiastical canticle, in the *allegro*, Bacchus' Feast (1818). As has been seen the choral conclusion was intended to be reserved for a *Tenth Symphony* and not for the *Ninth Symphony*.
Later he said that he wished to accomplish in his *Tenth Symphony* "the reconciliation of the modern world with the ancient, which Goethe had attempted in his *Second Faust*."
[2]   The subject is the legend of a horseman who is loved and captured by a fairy, and who suffers from nostalgia and lack of liberty. There are analogies between this poem and that of *Tannhäuser*. Beethoven worked at it between 1823 and 1826. (See A. Ehrhard *Franz Grillparzer*, 1900).
[3]   Since 1808 Beethoven had made plans for writing the music to *Faust* (The first part of *Faust* appeared under the title of *Tragedy* in the autumn of 1807). It was then his dearest plan.

travel. [1]

Dr. Spiker, who saw him in 1826, said that his face had become smiling and jovial. The same year when Grillparzer spoke to him for the last time, it was Beethoven who had more energy than the worn-out poet: "Ah!" said the latter, "if I had a thousandth part of your strength and determination." Times were hard; the monarchial reaction oppressed their spirits. "The censors have killed me," groaned Grillparzer. "One must go to North America if one wishes to speak freely." But no power could put a stop to Beethoven's thoughts. "Words are bound in chains, but, happily, sounds are still free," poet Kuffner wrote to him. Beethoven's is the great voice of freedom, perhaps the only one then of the whole of German thought. He felt it. Often he spoke of the duty which was imposed on him to act by means of his art "for poor humanity, for humanity to come, to restore its courage and to shake off its lassitude and cowardice." "At the present time," he wrote to his nephew, "there is need for mighty spirits to lash into action these wretched rebellious human souls." Dr. Müller said in 1827 that "Beethoven always expressed himself freely on the subjects of government, the police, the aristocracy, even in public. The police knew him but they looked on his

---

[1] "The South of France! It is there, there!" (from a notebook in the Berlin Library). "To go away from here. Only on this sole condition will you be able to rise again to the high level of your art.... A Symphony, then to go away, away, away. The summer to work during a voyage.... Then to travel in Italy and Sicily with some other artist."

criticisms and satires as harmless fancies, and they did not care to interfere with the man whose genius had such an extraordinary reputation."[1]

Thus nothing was able to break this indomitable will. It seemed now to make sport of grief. The music written in these last years, in spite of the painful circumstances under which it was composed, [2] has often quite a new, ironical character of heroic and joyous disdain. The very last piece that he finished, the new *Finale* to the *Quartet, Op.* 130, is very gay. This was in November 1826, four months before his death. In truth this gaiety is not of the usual kind; for at times it is the harsh and spasmodic laughter of which Moscheles speaks; often it is the affecting smile, the result of suffering conquered. It matters not; he is the conqueror. He does not believe in death.

It came, however. At the end of November, 1826, he caught a chill which turned to pleurisy: he was taken ill in

---

[1]   In 1819 he was followed by the police for having said aloud "That, after all, Christ was only a crucified Jew." He was then writing the *Mass in D.* That work alone is enough to show the freedom of his religious inspirations. (For the religious opinions of Beethoven, see Theodor von Frimmel; *Beethoven*, 3rd Edition, Verlag Harmonié; and *Beethovenia*, edited Georg Müller, Vol. II, Blöchinger). No less free in politics, Beethoven boldly attacked the vices of the government. He attacked amongst other things, the administration of justice, hindered by the slowness of its process, the stupid police regulations, the rude and lazy clerks in office, who killed all individual initiative and paralysed all action: the unfair privileges of a degenerate aristocracy, the high taxation, etc. His political sympathies seemed to be with England at that time.

[2]   The suicide of his nephew.

Vienna when returning from a journey undertaken in winter to arrange for the future of his nephew. [1] He was far from his friends. He told his nephew to go for a doctor. The wretch forgot his commission and only remembered two days after. The doctor came too late and treated Beethoven unskillfully. For three months his iron constitution fought against the illness. On January 3rd, 1827, he made his well-loved nephew his chief executor. He thought of his dear friends on the Rhine; he wrote again to Wegeler: "How I would like to talk with you! But I am too weak. I can do no more than embrace you in my heart, you and your Lorchen." Poverty would have made his last moments more gloomy, had it not been for the generosity of some English friends. He had become very gentle and very patient. [2] On his death-bed on February 17th, 1827, after three operations and awaiting a fourth, [3] he wrote with perfect calmness, "I am patient and I think that all misfortune brings some blessing with it."

This boon was deliverance—"the end of the comedy," as

---

[1] See an article by Dr. Klotz Forest on the last illness and death of Beethoven in the *Chronique Médicale* of April 1st and 15th, 1906. There is also exact information in the conversation books where the doctor's questions are written down, and in the article of the doctor himself (Dr. Wawruch) in the *Vienna Times*, in 1842.

[2] The recollections of the singer, Ludwig Cramolini, which have been published, relate a touching visit to Beethoven during his last illness. He found Beethoven possessed of a calm serenity, a touching kindness. (See the *Frankfurter Zeitung*, of September 29th, 1907).

[3] The operations took place on December 20th, January 8th, February 2nd, and February 27th.

he said when dying. We might say rather the end of the *tragedy*....

He died in the climax of a violent storm, a tempest of snow, heavily punctuated with terrible thunder claps. A strange hand closed his eyes,[1] March 26th, 1827.

Beloved Beethoven! So many others have praised his artistic grandeur. But he is easily the first of musicians. He is the most heroic soul in modern art. He is the grandest and the best friend of those who suffer and struggle. When we are saddened by worldly miseries, it is he who comes near to us, as he used to go and play to a mother in grief, and without uttering a word thus console her by the song of his own plaintive resignation. And when we are utterly exhausted in the eternal battle uselessly waged against mediocrity, vice and virtue, it is an unspeakable boon to find fresh strength in this great ocean-torrent of strong will and faith. An atmosphere of courage emanates

---

[1]   The young musician, Anselm Huttenbrenner. "God be praised," said Breuning. "Let us thank Him for having put an end to this long and pitiful martyrdom."

All Beethoven's MSS. books and furniture were sold by auction for 1,575 florins. The catalogue contained 252 lots of manuscripts and musical books which did not exceed the sum of 982 florins 37 kreutzer. The *conversation-books* and the *Tagebucher* were sold for 1 florin 20 kreutzer. Amongst his books Beethoven possessed: Kant's *Natural Science and Astronomy*; Bode's *Knowledge of the Heavens*; Thomas à Kempis' *The Imitation of Christ*. The Censor confiscated Seum's *Walks round Syracuse*, Kotzebue's *Over the Adel*, and Fessler's *Views on Religion and Theology*.

from his personality, a love of battle, [1] the exultation of a conscious feeling of the *God within*. It seems that in his constant communion with nature [2] he had ended by assimilating its deep and mighty powers. Grillparzer, who admired Beethoven with a kind of awe, said of him, "He penetrated into regions where art melts away and unites with the wild and capricious elements." Schumann wrote similarly of his *Symphony in C minor*. "Every time it is performed it exercises an unvarying power on us, like natural phenomena which fill us with awe and amazement every time they occur." And Schindler, his confidential friend, says, "He possessed the spirit of nature." It is true, "Beethoven is a force of nature; and this battle of elemental power against the rest of nature is a spectacle of truly Homeric grandeur."

His whole life is like a stormy day. At the beginning—a fresh clear morning, perhaps a languid breeze, scarcely a breath of air. But there is already in the still air a secret menace, a dark foreboding. Large shadows loom and pass; tragic rumblings; murmuring awesome silences; the furious gusts of the winds of the *Eroica* and the *C minor*. However, the freshness of the day is not yet gone. Joy remains joy; the brightness of the sky is not overcast; sadness is never without a ray of hope. But

---

[1] "I am always happy when I have to master some difficulty" (Letter to the Immortal Loved One). "I should like to live a thousand lives.... I am not suited for a quiet life" (To Wegeler, November 16th, 1801).

[2] "Beethoven talked to me on the science of nature and helped me with this study as with music. It was not the laws of nature but its elementary powers that attracted him." (Schindler).

after 1810 the poise of the soul is disturbed. A strange light glows. Mists obscure his deepest thoughts; some of the clearer thoughts appear as vapour rising; they disappear, are dispelled, yet form anew; they obscure the heart with their melancholy and capricious gloom; often the musical idea seems to vanish entirely, to be submerged, but only to re-appear again at the end of a piece in a veritable storm of melody. Even joy has assumed a rough and riotous character. A bitter feeling becomes mingled in all his sentiments. [1] Storms gather as evening comes on. Heavy clouds are big with tempests. Lightning flashes o'er the black of night. The climax of the hurricane is approaching. Suddenly, at the height of the tempest, the darkness is dispersed. Night is driven away and the clear, tranquil atmosphere is restored by a sheer act of will power.

What a conquest was this! What Napoleonic battle can be likened to it? What was Austerlitz glory to the radiance of this superhuman effort, this victory, the most brilliant that has ever been won by an infirm and lonely spirit. Sorrow personified, to whom the world refused joy, created joy himself to give to the world. He forged it from his own misery, as he proudly said in reviewing his life. And indeed it was the motto of his whole heroic soul:

JOY THROUGH SUFFERING

(To Countess Erdödy, October 19th, 1815).

---

[1] "Oh, how good life is; but mine is for ever embittered." (Letter to Wegeler, May 2nd, 1810).

Bust of Beethoven by Hugo Hagen, 1892

HIS WILL

(A Lichnowsky, 21 septembre 1814)

Alone, Alone, Alone

(To Lichnovsky, 21 Sept., 1814).

THE HEILIGENSTADT WILL.[1]

For my brothers KARL and JOHANN.

O ye men who regard or declare me to be malignant, stubborn or cynical, how unjust are ye towards me! You do not know the secret cause of my seeming so. From childhood onward, my heart and mind prompted me to be kind and tender, and I was ever inclined to accomplish great deeds. But only think that during the last six years I have been in a wretched condition, rendered worse by unintelligent physicians. Deceived from year to year with hopes of improvement, and then finally forced to the prospect of *lasting infirmity* (which may last for years, or even be totally incurable). Born with a fiery, active temperament, even susceptive of the diversions of society, I had soon to retire from the world, to live a solitary life. At times, even, I endeavoured to forget all this, but how harshly was I driven back by the redoubled experience of my bad hearing. Yet it was not possible for me to say to men: "Speak louder, shout,

---

[1] Translation by J. S. Shedlock.

for I am deaf." Alas! how could I declare the weakness of a *sense* which in me *ought to be* more acute than in others—a sense which *formerly* I possessed in highest perfection, a perfection such as few in my profession enjoy, or ever have enjoyed; no, I cannot do it. Forgive, therefore, if you see me withdraw, when I would willingly mix with you. My misfortune pains me doubly, in that I am certain to be misunderstood. For me there can be no recreation in the society of my fellow creatures, no refined conversations, no interchange of thought. Almost alone, and only mixing in society when absolutely necessary, I am compelled to live as an exile. If I approach near to people, a feeling of hot anxiety comes over me lest my condition should be noticed—for so it was during these past six months which I spent in the country. Ordered by my intelligent physician to spare my hearing as much as possible, he almost fell in with my present frame of mind, although many a time I was carried away by my sociable inclinations. But how humiliating was it, when some one standing close to me heard a distant flute, and I heard *nothing*, or a *shepherd singing*, and again I heard nothing. Such incidents almost drove me to despair; at times I was on the point of putting an end to my life—*art* alone restrained my hand. Oh! it seemed as if I could not quit this earth until I had produced all I felt within me, and so I continued this wretched life, wretched indeed, with so sensitive a body that a somewhat sudden change can throw me from the best into the worst state. *Patience*, I am told, I must choose as my guide. I have done so—

lasting, I hope, will be my resolution to bear up until it pleases the inexorable Parcae to break the thread. Forced, already in my 28th year,[①] to become a philosopher it is not easy; for an artist more difficult than for any one else.

O Divine Being, Thou Who lookest down into my inmost soul, Thou understandest, Thou knowest that love for mankind and a desire to do good dwell therein. Oh, my fellow men, when one day you read this, remember that you were unjust to me, and let the unfortunate one console himself if he can find one like himself, who in spite of all obstacles which nature has thrown in his way, has still done everything in his power to be received into the ranks of worthy artists and men.

You, my brothers Karl and Johann, as soon as I am dead, beg Professor Schmidt, if he be still living, to describe my malady, and annex this written account to that of my illness, so that at least the world may know, so far as it is possible, may become reconciled to me after my death. And now I declare you both heirs to my small fortune (if such it may be called). Divide it honourably and dwell in peace, and help each other. What you have done against me, has, as you know, long been forgiven. And you, brother Karl, I especially thank you for the attachment you have shown towards me of late. My prayer is that your life may be better, less troubled by cares than mine. Recommend to

---

① Beethoven was at the time in his 32nd year; but he never knew precisely his age.

your children virtue; it alone can bring happiness, not money. I speak from experience. It was virtue which bore me up in time of trouble; to her, next to my art, I owe thanks for my not having laid violent hands on myself. Farewell, and love one another. My thanks to all friends, especially *Prince Lichnovsky and Professor Schmidt.* I should much like one of you to keep as an heirloom the instruments given to me by Prince L., but let no strife arise between you concerning them; if money should be of more service to you, just sell them. How happy I feel that even when lying in my grave I may be useful to you.

So let it be. I joyfully hasten to meet death. If it come before I have had opportunity to develop all my artistic faculties, it will come, my hard fate notwithstanding, too soon, and I should probably wish it later—yet even then I shall be happy, for will it not deliver me from a state of endless suffering? Come when thou wilt, I shall face thee courageously; farewell, and when I am dead, do not entirely forget me. This I deserve from you, for during my lifetime I often thought of you, and how to make you happy. Be ye so.

LUDWIG VAN BEETHOVEN.

Heiglnstadt, the 6th of October, 1802.

(Black Seal).

On the fourth side of the large Will sheet:

Heiglnstadt, October, 1802, thus I take my farewell of thee—and, indeed, sadly—yes, that fond hope which I entertained when I came here, of being at any rate healed up to a certain point, must be entirely abandoned... As the leaves of autumn fall and fade, so it has withered away for me; almost the same as when I came here do I go away—even the high courage which often in the beautiful summer days quickened me, that has vanished. O Providence, let me have just one pure day of joy; so long is it since true joy filled my heart. Oh when, oh when, oh Divine Being, shall I be able once again to feel it in the temple of nature and of men? Never—no—that would be too hard.

For my brothers Karl and Johann to execute after my death.

CODICIL. TESTAMENTARY DISPOSITION.

My nephew, Karl, shall be my sole heir; the capital of my estate shall, however, descend to his natural heirs or to those appointed by him through a will.

Ludwig van Beethoven.

HIS LETTERS

BEETHOVEN AT THE AGE OF 44.

From an Engraving by Blasius Hoefel after the

Drawing by Louis Letronne, 1814.

BEETHOVEN'S LETTERS.[1]

I.

To KARL AMENDA at Wirben in Courland.

(Vienna, June 1, 1800)

My dear, my good Amenda, my heartily beloved friend.

With deep emotion, with mixed pain and pleasure did I receive and read your last letter. To what can I compare your fidelity, your attachment to me. Oh! how pleasant it is that you have always remained so kind to me; yes, I also know that you, of all men, are the most trustworthy. You are no *Viennese friend*; no, you are one of those such as my native country produces. How often do I wish you were with me, your Beethoven is most unhappy, and at strife with nature and Creator. The latter I have often cursed for exposing His creatures to the smallest

---

[1] For the Letters, I have been kindly allowed by Messrs. J. M. Dent & Co., to use Mr. J. S. Shedldck's splendid translation in his monumental, "*Letters of Ludwig van Beethoven*" (2 volumes, 1909), which contain no less than 7,220 documents.

chance, so that frequently the richest buds are thereby crushed and destroyed. Only think that the noblest part of me, my sense of hearing has become very weak. Already, when you were with me I noticed traces of it, and I said nothing. Now it has become worse, and it remains to be seen whether it can ever be healed.... I much fear that my hearing will not improve; maladies of that kind are the most difficult of all to cure. What a sad life I am now compelled to lead; I must avoid all that is near and dear to me, and then to be among such wretched egotistical beings such as... etc. I can say that among all, Lichnowski has best stood the test. Since last year he has settled on me 600 florins, which, together with the good sale of my works, enables me to live without anxiety. Everything I write I can sell immediately five times over, and also be well paid. I have composed a fair quantity, and as I hear you have ordered pianofortes from... I will send you many things in one of the packing cases so it will not cost you so very much.

Now to my consolation, a man has come here with whom intercourse is a pleasure, and whose friendship is free from all selfishness. He is one of the friends of my youth. I have often spoken to him about you, and told him that since I left my native country, you are the one whom my heart has chosen. Even he does not like the latter is and remains too weak for friendship. I consider him and... mere instruments on which when it pleases me I play; but they can never become noble witnesses of my inner and outer activity, nor be in true sympathy with me; I value them according as they are useful to me. Oh! how happy should I now be if I had my perfect hearing, for I should then hasten to you. As it is, I must in all things be behind-hand; my best years will slip away without bringing forth what, with my talent and my strength I ought to have accomplished. I must now have recourse to sad resignation. I have, it is true, resolved not to worry about all this but how is it possible? Yes, Amenda, if six months hence my malady is beyond cure, then I lay claim to your help. You must leave everything and come to me. I will travel (my malady interferes least with my playing and composition, most only in conversation), and you must be my companion. I am convinced good fortune will not fail me. With whom need I be afraid of measuring my strength? Since you went away I have written music of all kinds, including operas and sacred works.

Yes, do not refuse; help your friend to bear with his troubles, his infirmity. I have also greatly improved my pianoforte playing. I hope this journey may also turn to your advantage; afterwards you will always remain with me. I have duly received all your letters, and although I have only answered a few, you have been always in my mind, and my heart, as always, beats tenderly for you. *Please keep as a great secret what I have told you about my hearing; trust no one, whoever it may be, with it.* Do write frequently; your letters, however short they may be, console me, do me good. I expect soon to get another one from you, my dear friend. Don't lend out my Quartet any more, because I have made many changes in it. I have only just learnt how to write quartets properly, as you will see when you receive them.

Now, my dear good friend, farewell! If, perchance, you believe that I can show you any kindness here, I need not of course, remind you to first address yourself to

Your faithful, truly loving,
L. V. BEETHOVEN.

II.

To Dr. F. WEGELER in Bonn.

Vienna, June 29, 1801

My good, dear Wegeler.

I am most grateful to you for thinking of me; I have so little deserved it, or sought to deserve it at your hands. And yet you are so very good, and are not kept back by anything, not even by my unpardonable negligence, but always remain a faithful, good, honest friend. That I could ever forget you, and especially all of you who were so kind and affectionate to me, no, do not believe it; there are moments in which I myself long for you—yes, and wish to spend some time with you. My native land, the beautiful country in which I first saw the light of the world, is ever as beautiful and distinct before mine eyes as when I left you. In short, I shall regard that time as one of the happiest of my life, when I see you again, and can greet our father Rhine. When that will be I cannot yet say. This much will I tell you, that you will only see me again when I am really great; not only greater as an artist, but as a man you shall find me better, more perfect; and if in our native land there are any signs of returning prosperity, I will only use my art for the benefit of the poor. O, happy moment, how fortunate I think myself in being able to get a fatherland created here!

You want to know something about my present state; well,

at present, it is not so bad. Since last year, Lichnowsky, who, however incredible it may seem when I tell it you, was always my warmest friend, and has remained so (of course, there have been slight misunderstandings between us, but just these have strengthened our friendship), has settled a fixed sum of 600 florins on me, and I can draw it so long as I fail to find a suitable post. My compositions are bringing in a goodly sum, and I may add, it is scarcely possible for me to execute the orders given. Also, for every work I have six, seven publishers, and if I choose, even more. They do not bargain with me; I demand and they pay. You see how pleasant it is. For example, I see a friend in distress, and if my purse do not allow of my helping him, I have only to sit down and in a short time he is relieved. Also I am more economical than I was formerly. If I should settle here, I shall certainly contrive to get one day every year for concerts, of which I have given some.

Only my envious demon, my bad health, has thrown obstacles in my way. For instance, my hearing has become weaker during the last three years, and this infirmity was in the first instance caused by my general health, which, as you know, was already, in the past, in a wretched state. Frank wished to restore me to health by means of strengthening medicines, and to cure my deafness by means of oil of almonds, but, *prosit!* nothing came of these remedies; my hearing became worse and worse, and my ill-health always remained in its first state. This continued until the autumn of last year, and ofttimes

I was in despair. Then an Asinus of a doctor advised cold baths; a more skillful one, the usual tepid Danube baths. These worked wonders; the state of my health improved, my deafness remained, or became worse. This winter I was truly miserable. I had terrible attacks of colic, and I fell quite back into my former state. So I remained for about four weeks and then went to Vering, for I thought that this state required medical aid, and in addition I had always placed faith in him. He ordered tepid Danube baths, and whenever I took one I had to pour into it a little bottle full of strengthening stuff. He gave me no medicine until about four days ago, when he ordered an application of herbs for the ear. And through these I can say I feel stronger and better; only the humming in my ears continues day and night without ceasing. I may truly say that my life is a wretched one. For the last two years I have avoided all society, for it is impossible for me to say to people "I am deaf." Were my profession any other it would not so much matter, but in my profession it is a terrible thing; and my enemies, of whom they are not a few, what would they say to this?

To give you an idea of this extraordinary deafness, I will tell you that when at the theatre, I am obliged to lean forward close to the orchestra, in order to understand what is being said on the stage. When somewhat at a distance I cannot hear the high tones of instruments, voices. In speaking it is not surprising that there are people who have never noticed it, for as a rule I am absent-minded, and they account for it in that way. Often I can scarcely hear anyone speaking to me; the tones, yes, but not the actual words; yet as soon as anyone shouts, it is unbearable. What will come of all this, heaven only knows! Vering says that there will *certainly be an improvement, though perhaps not a perfect cure.* I have, indeed, often—cursed my existence; Plutarch taught resignation. If nothing else is possible I will defy my fate, although there will be moments in my life when I shall be God's most wretched creature. I beg you not to tell anyone about this; don't say even a word to Lorchen. I only tell it you as a secret; I should be glad if you would open up correspondence with Vering on the subject. Should my present state continue, I would come next spring to you. You would take a house for me in some beautiful place in the country, and so I would rusticate for six months. By that means there might come a change. Resignation! what a miserable refuge, and yet it is the only way for me. Pray forgive me for telling you of a friend's trouble, when you yourself are in sad circumstances.

Stephen Breuning is now here, and we are together almost daily. It does me good to hark back to old times. He is really a good, noble young fellow, who knows a thing or two, and whose heart, as with all of us more or less, is sound. I have very fine rooms now, which look on to the bastion, and this for my health is of double value. I really think I can arrange for Breuning to come and live with me. You shall have your Antiochus, and a rare lot of my new compositions, unless you think it will cost you too much. Honestly speaking, your love for art gives me the highest pleasure. Only write to me how it is to be managed, and I will send you all my works, of which the number is now pretty large and it is daily increasing. In place of the portrait of my grandfather, which I beg you to send as soon as possible by stage coach, I send you that of his grandson, your ever good and affectionate Beethoven. It is coming out here at Artaria's, who, also other art firms, have often asked me for it. I will write shortly to Stoffel, and read him a bit of a lecture about his cross temper. He shall hear what I have to say about old friendship, he shall promise on his oath not to grieve you any more in your, apart from this, sad circumstances.

I will also write to kind Lorchen. I have never forgot a single one of you, my dear good people, although you never get any news from me; but writing, as you well know, was never a strong point with me—years, even, have passed without my best friends ever receiving anything. I only live in my music, and I have scarcely begun one thing when I start another. As I am now working, I am often engaged on three or four things at the same time.

Write often to me now; I will see to it that I find time sometimes to write to you. Greetings to all, also to the good wife of the privy councillor, and tell her that I still, occasionally, have a "raptus." I am not surprised at the change in K; fortune is fickle, and does not always fall to the most worthy, the best. A word about Ries, to whom hearty greetings. As regards his son, about whom I will write shortly, although I am of opinion that to make his way in the world, Paris is better than Vienna. The latter city is overcrowded, and even persons of the highest merit find it hard to maintain themselves. By the autumn, or the winter, I will see what I can do for him, for then every one is returning.

Farewell, good, faithful Wegeler. Rest assured of the love and friendship of

Your,

BEETHOVEN.

III.

To Dr. FRANZ WEGELER in Bonn.

November 16 (1801 ?)

My good Wegeler.

I thank you for the fresh proof of your anxiety concerning myself, and all the more as I am so little deserving of it. You want to know how I am, what I am taking; and however unwillingly I may discuss the matter, I certainly like best to do it with you.

For the last few months, Vering has ordered herb plasters to be constantly placed on both arms; and these, as you will know, are composed of a certain bark. This is a most unpleasant cure, as, until the bark has sufficiently drawn, I am deprived for a day or so of the free use of my arms, to say nothing of the pain. I cannot, it is true, deny that the humming with which my deafness actually began, has become somewhat weaker, especially in the left ear. My hearing, however, has not in the least improved; I really am not quite sure whether it has not become worse. My general health is better, and especially after I have taken luke warm baths a few times, I am fairly well for eight or ten days. I seldom take any tonic; I am now applying herb-plasters according to your advice. Vering won't hear of shower baths, but I am really very dissatisfied with him; he shows so little care and forbearance for such a malady if I did not actually go to him, and that costs me a great effort, I should never see him. What is your opinion of Schmidt? I do not like making a change, yet it seems to me that Vering is too much a practitioner to be able to take in new ideas through books. Schmidt appears to me a very different kind of man, and perhaps would not be so remiss. I hear wonders of galvanism; what do you say about it? A doctor told me he had seen a deaf and dumb child in Berlin who had recovered his hearing, also a man who had been deaf for seven years. I have just heard that your Schmidt is making experiments with it.

My life is again somewhat pleasanter, for I mix in society. You can scarcely imagine what a dreary, sad life I have led during the past two years. My weak hearing always seemed to me like a ghost and I ran away from people, was forced to appear a misanthrope, though not at all in my character. This change has been brought about by an enchanting maiden, who loves me, and whom I love. Again during the past two years I have had some happy moments, and for the first time I feel that marriage can bring happiness. Unfortunately, she is not of my station in life, and now—for the moment I certainly could not marry—I must bravely bustle about. If it were not for my hearing, I should already long ago have travelled half over the world, and that I must do. For me there is no greater pleasure than that of practising and displaying my art. Do not believe that I should feel happy among you. What, indeed, could make me happier? Even your solicitude would pain me; at every moment I should read pity on your faces, and that would make me still more miserable. My beautiful native country, what was my lot when there? Nothing but hope of a better state, and, except for this evil, I should already have won it! O that I could be free from it, and encompass the world! My youth, yes I feel it, is only now beginning; have I not always been sickly? My strength, both of body and mind, for some time has been on the increase. Every day I approach nearer to the goal; this I feel, though I can scarcely describe it. Only through this, can your Beethoven live. Don't talk of rest! I know no other but sleep, and sorry enough am I, that I am compelled to give more time to it than formerly. If only half freed from my infirmity, then— as a thorough, ripe man—I will come to you and renew the old feelings of friendship.

You will see me as happy as my lot can be here below, not unhappy. No, that I could not endure; I will seize fate by the throat; it shall certainly never wholly overcome me. Oh! life is so beautiful, would I could have a thousand lives! I feel I am no longer fit to lead a quiet life! Do write as soon as you can. See to it that Stephen makes up his mind to get an appointment in the Order of German Knights.

For his health, life here is too fatiguing. And besides, he leads such a retired life, that I do not see how he can get on. You know how it is here; I do not mean to say that society would render him less languid; he can never be persuaded to go into it. Some time ago I had a musical party at my house; but our friend Stephen did not turn up. Do advise him to take more rest and to be more steady. I have done all I could; without he takes this advice, he can never become either happy or healthy. Now, tell me in your next letter, whether it matters if I send you a great deal of my music. What you really don't want you can sell, and so you will have your postage—also my portrait. Best remembrances to Lorchen—also Mamma—and Christoph. You do really love me a little, do you not? Be as well assured of this (of my love), as of the friendship of your

BEETHOVEN.

IV.

Letter from Wegeler and Eleonore von Breuning to Beethoven.

Coblentz, 28 December, 1825.

My dear old Louis.

I cannot allow one of Ries' ten children to leave Vienna without recalling him to your remembrance. If during the twenty-eight years since I left Vienna, you have not received a long letter from me every two months, you must put it down to your own silence after the first letters which I sent you. It should not be so and especially now that we other old people live so entirely in the past and derive our chief pleasure in recollections of our youth. For me at least, my acquaintance and my firm friendship to you, thanks to your good mother whom God now blesses, is a guiding star in my life, towards which I turn with pleasure.... I raise my eyes to you as to a hero, and I am proud to be able to say: "I have had some influence on his development; he confided in me his ambitions and his dreams; and when later he was so often misunderstood, I knew quite well what he wanted." God be praised that I have been able to speak of you with my wife, and now with my children! My mother-in-law's house was more your home than your own home, especially after the death of your good mother. Tell us still once more, "I think of you both in joy and in sorrow." A man, even when he has risen as high as you, is only happy once in his life: when he is young. Your thoughts should hark back happily many times to the stones of Bonn, Godesburg, Pépinière, etc.

Now I want to speak of myself, of ourselves, to give you an example of how you ought to reply to me.

After my return from Vienna in 1796, things went rather badly with me. For a long time I had to rely for a living on my consultations as a doctor, and that lasted for several years in this wretched country, before I could even make a bare livelihood. Then I became a professor with a salary, and I married. A year later I had a daughter who is still living and who is quite accomplished. In addition to a very clear head, she has the quiet ways of her father; and she plays admirably some of Beethoven's Sonatas. She can claim no merit for this, for it is an inborn gift with her. In 1807 I had a son who is now studying medicine in Berlin. In four years I shall send him to Vienna. Will you look after him for me? I celebrated, in August, my 60th birthday by a party of sixty friends and acquaintances, including the chief people of Bonn. I have lived here since 1807, and have a fine house and a good position. My superiors are satisfied with me, and the King has given me some orders and medals. Lore and I are content. Now that I have told you all about ourselves, it is your turn....

Do you never wish to turn your eyes from the tower of St. Stephen's? Has travel no charms for you? Do you never wish to see the Rhine again? With every good wish from Madam Lore and myself,

Your very old friend,

WEGELER.

Dear Beethoven—dear for such a long time!

It was my wish that Wegeler should write to you again. Now that this is done, I should like to add a few words— not only to recall myself to your remembrance, but to renew the pressing question whether you have not a desire to see the Rhine and your birthplace again, and to give Wegeler and me the greatest joy possible. Our Lenchen thanks you for so many happy hours; she delights in hearing us speak of you; she knows all the little adventures of our happy youthful days at Bonn—of the quarrel and the reconciliation.... How happy she would be to see you! Unfortunately, the little one has no special aptitude for music; but she has done so much by application and perseverance that she can play your Sonatas, Variations, etc.; and as music is always the greatest relaxation for Wegeler, she is thus able to give him many happy hours. Julius has some talent for music, but up to the present it has been neglected; for the last six months, he has been learning the violoncello with zest and pleasure; and as he has a good teacher in Berlin I believe that he will get on well. The two children are tall and resemble their father; they also possess that fine cheery disposition which Wegeler, thanks to God, has not even yet lost.... He takes great pleasure in playing the themes of your Variations; the old ones have the greater preference, but he often plays the new ones, too, with incredible patience. Your *Opferlied* is placed above everything. Wegeler never goes to his room without putting it on the piano. So, dear Beethoven, you can see how lasting and real a thing is the remembrance which we always have of you! Tell us then just once that this is not worthless to you, and that we are not quite forgotten. If it were not so difficult to do as one wishes, we should already have been to Vienna to see my brother, and have the pleasure of seeing you again; but such a journey is out of the question now that our son is at Berlin. Wegeler has told you how everything goes with us—we should do wrong to complain. Even the most difficult times have been better for us than for hundreds of others. The greatest blessing is that we all keep well and that we have such good and noble children. Yes, they have hardly given us any trouble, and they are such merry and happy little people. Lenchen has had only one great grief; it was when our poor Burscheid died: a loss none of us will ever forget. Adieu, dear Beethoven, and think of us as the most loyal of friends.

ELN. WEGELER.

V

To Dr. FRANZ WEGELER.

Vienna, 7th October, 1826.

My dear old friend.

I cannot tell you how much pleasure your letter and that of your Lorchen gave me. Certainly, a reply ought to have been sent with lightning speed, but I am generally somewhat careless about writing, because I think that the better sort of men know me without this. I often compose the answer in my mind, but when I wish to write it down, I usually throw the pen away, because I cannot write as I feel. I remember all the love which you have constantly shown me, for instance, when you had my room whitewashed, and so pleasantly surprised me. It is the same with the Breuning family. If we were separated, that happened in the natural course of things; every one must pursue and try to attain distinction in his calling; but the eternal unshaken foundations of virtue held us ever firmly united. Unfortunately, I cannot write to you to-day so much as I wished, as I am bedridden, and therefore confine myself to answering certain points of your letter.

You write that I am somewhere spoken of as a natural son of the late King of Prussia; I, likewise, heard of this long ago, but have made it a principle never to write anything about myself, nor to reply to anything written about me. So I willingly leave it to you to make known to the world the uprightness of my parents, and especially of my mother. You write about your son. I need not say that if he comes here he will find in me a friend and father, and if I can help, or be of service to him in any way, I will gladly do so.

I still have the silhouette of your Lorchen, from which you will see that all the goodness and affection shown to me in my youth are still dear to me.

Of my diplomas, I will only tell you briefly, that I am honorary member of the Royal Society of Sciences of Sweden, as well as of Amsterdam, and also honorary citizen of Vienna. A short time ago a certain Dr. Spiker took with him my last great Symphony with chorus to Berlin; it is dedicated to the King, and I had to write the dedication with my own hand. I had already sought permission through the Embassy to be allowed to dedicate this work to the King, and it was granted. At Dr. Spiker's instigation, I was obliged myself to hand over to him the manuscript for the King, with the corrections in my own handwriting, as it was to be placed in the Royal Library. Something has been said to me about the red order of the Eagle, 2nd class; what will come of it, I do not know, for I have never sought such tokens of honour; yet in these times, they would not be unwelcome to me for many reasons.

Moreover, my motto is always: "Nulla dies sine linea," and if I ever let the Muse sleep, it is only that she may awaken all the stronger. I hope still to bring some great works into the world, and then, like an old child, to end my earthly career amongst good men.

You will also soon receive some music from Schott Brothers of Mainz. The portrait which you receive enclosed, is certainly an artistic masterpiece, but it is not the last which has been taken of me. With regard to tokens of honour, which I know will give you pleasure, I may also mention that a medal was sent to me by the late King of France with the inscription: "*Donné par le Roi à Monsieur Beethoven*," accompanied by a very obliging letter from the *premier gentilhomme du Roi Duc de Châtres*.

My dear friend, for to-day, farewell. For the rest, the remembrance of the past takes hold of me, and not without many tears will you receive this letter. A beginning is now made, and you will soon get another letter, and the more frequently you write, the more pleasure will you give me. No inquiry is necessary on either side concerning our friendship; and so, farewell. I beg you to kiss and embrace your dear Lorchen and the children in my name, and at the same time to think of me. God be with you all.

As always, your true friend who honours you,

BEETHOVEN.

VI.

To Dr. F. G. WEGELER in Bonn.

Vienna, February 17, 1827.

Fortunately I received your second letter through Breuning. I am still too weak to answer it, but you may believe me that everything in it is welcome and desirable. My recovery, if I may call it so, is very slow; a fourth operation is to be expected, although the doctors do not say anything about it. I am patiently thinking that every evil has sometimes its good. But now I am astonished to see from your last letter that you have not received anything. From the present letter you will perceive that I wrote to you already on the tenth of December last year. With the portrait, it is the same, as you will see from the date when you receive it. "Frau Steffen said," [1] in short, Stephen wished to send you these things if some opportunity offered, but they remained lying here up to this date; moreover until now, it was difficult to send them back. You will now get the portrait by post, through Schott and Co., who also send you the music. I should like to tell you still much more, but I am too weak, thus I can only embrace you and your Lorchen in spirit.

With true friendship and affection to you and yours, I am

Your old, true friend,

BEETHOVEN.

---

[1]   Quotation from a well-known song.

VII.

To I. MOSCHELES in London.

Vienna, March 14, 1827.

My dear Moscheles.

Some days ago I found out through Herr Lewinger that you inquired in a letter to him of the 10th of February regarding the state of my illness, of which so many different rumours have been spread about. Although I have no doubts whatever that my letter of the 24th of February has arrived, which will explain everything you desire to know, I can but thank you for your sympathy with my sad lot, and beseech you to be solicitous about the request which you know of from my first letter, and I am quite convinced that, in union with Sir Smart and other of my friends, you will succeed in bringing about a favourable result for me at the Philharmonic Society. I have once more written to Sir Smart about it.

On the 27th of February I underwent the fourth operation, and there are visible symptoms that I shall have to suffer a fifth. What does it tend to, and what will become of me if it continues for some time longer? A hard lot, indeed, has fallen upon me! However, I submit to the will of fate, and only pray to God so to ordain it in His divine will, that I may be protected from want as long as I have to endure death in life. This will give me strength to bear my lot, however terrible it may be, with humble submission to the will of the Most High.

Therefore, my dear Moscheles, I entrust once more my affair to you, and remain with greatest respect ever

Your friend,

L. VAN BEETHOVEN.

Hummel is here and has called on me several times.

Drawing by Enrico Caruso, 1910

HIS THOUGHTS

PAGE OF AUTOGRAPH OF "MOONLIGHT" SONATA.

IN BEETHOVEN'S HOUSE AT BONN.

ON MUSIC

"Il n'y a pas de règle qu'on ne peut blesser à cause de SCHÖNER" (There is no rule which one cannot break for the sake of BEAUTY).

"Music ought to create and fan the fire of the spirit of man."

"Music is a higher revelation than the whole of wisdom and the whole of philosophy.... He who penetrates the meaning of my music shall be freed from all the misery which afflicts others."

(To Bettina, 1810.)

"There is nothing finer than to approach the Divine and to shed its rays on the human race."

"Why do I write? What I have in my heart must come out;

and that is why I compose."

"Do you believe that I think of a divine violin when the spirit speaks to me and that I write what it dictates?"

(To Schuppanzigh.)

"According to my usual manner of composing, even in my instrumental music, I always have the whole in my mind; here, however, that whole is to a certain extent divided, and I have afresh to think myself into the music."

(To Treitschke: from correspondence concerning Beethoven's musical settings to some of his poems. Treitschke was the man who revised the libretto of Fidelio when it was seriously thought of reviving it.)

"One should compose without a piano. The faculty of expressing what one desires and feels (which is so essential a need to noble natures) comes only by degrees."

(To the Archduke Rudolph.)

"The descriptions of a picture belong to painting; even the poet in this matter may, in comparison with my art, esteem himself lucky, for his domain in this respect is not so limited as mine, yet the latter extends further into other regions, and to attain to our kingdom is not easy."

(To Wilhelm Gerhardi in Leipzig from Nussdorf, July, 1817.)

"Liberty and progress are the goals of art just as of life in general. If we are not as solid as the old masters, the refinement of civilization has at least enlarged our out-look."

(To the Archduke Rudolph.)

"I am not in the habit of altering my compositions when they are once finished. I have never done this, for I hold firmly that the slightest change alters the character of the composition."

(To George Thomson, publisher, Edinburgh.)

"Pure Church music ought to be performed entirely *by the voices only*, except for the *Gloria* or words of that kind. That is why I prefer Palestrina; but it would be absurd to imitate him without possessing his spirit and his religious convictions."

(To the organist Freudenberg.)

"When your piano pupil has the proper fingering, the exact rhythm and plays the notes correctly, pay attention only to the style; do not stop for little faults or make remarks on them until the end of the piece. This method produces *musicians*, which after all is one of the chief aims of musical art.... For the passage work (virtuosity) make him use all the fingers freely.... Doubtless by employing fewer fingers a 'pearly' effect is obtained—as it is put—'like a pearl.' But one likes other jewels at times."

(To Czerny.)

(The Baron de Trémont wrote in 1809, "Beethoven's piano playing was not very correct and his manner of fingering was often faulty; the quality of his tone was not beyond reproach. But who could dream of the player? One was completely absorbed by the thoughts which his hands tried to express as well as they could.")

"Amongst the old masters, only Handel and Sebastian Bach had true genius."

(To the Archduke Rudolph, 1819.)

"My heart beats in entire concord with the lofty and grand art of Sebastian Bach, that patriarch of harmony (*dieses Urvaters der Harmonie*)."

(To Hofmeister, 1801.)

"I have always been one of the greatest admirers of Mozart, and I shall remain so until my latest breath."

(To the Abbé Stadler, 1826.)

"I admire your works above all other pieces for the theatre. I am in ecstasy each time I hear a new work by you, and I take more interest in them than in my own. In brief, I admire you and I love you.... *You will always remain the one I esteem most amongst all my contemporaries. If you wish to give me an extreme pleasure do write me a few lines. That would give me great satisfaction. Art unites everybody, how much more true artists, and perhaps you will consider me also worthy of being counted one of this number."*

(To Cherubini, 1823.)

(The words in italics are in French in the original with some defective spelling. This letter to Cherubini was not answered.)

ON CRITICISM

"In all that concerns me as an artist, no one has ever heard me say that I pay the least attention to what has been written about me."

(To Schott, 1825.)

"I think with Voltaire that mere fly-stings will not hold back a run-away horse."

(1826.)

"As for these idiots, one can only let them talk. Their prattling will certainly not make anyone immortal, any more than it will raise to immortality any of those whom Apollo has destined for it."

(1801.)